Fly Fishing the Madison

Fly Fishing the Madison

by Craig Mathews and Gary LaFontaine

THE LYONS PRESS
Guilford, Connecticut
An imprint of The Globe Pequot Press

The Lyons Press is an imprint of The Globe Pequot Press.

10 9 8 7 6 5 4 3

Printed in the United States of America

Originally published in 2001 by Greycliff Publishing Company.

ISBN-13: 978-1-58574-507-4
ISBN-10: 1-58574-507-3

Library of Congress Cataloging-in-Publication Data is available on file.

To the Montana Land Reliance, Montana Trout Foundation, Nature Conservancy of Montana, Trout Unlimited, River Network, Trust for Public Lands, and other organizations and their members who love rivers and work hard to protect them and wild trout. These groups help secure conservation easements that forever protect wild trout habitat and keep the land intact and free from subdivisions. Support them!

CONTENTS

ILLUSTRATIONS

Key Flies

PREFACE
BY GARY LAFONTAINE

*T*his book started out as several hours of recorded interview between its authors—more of a conversation, really, that took advantage of two persons' combined experience on the Madison River in Yellowstone National Park and Montana. Craig Mathews has fished, guided, and created flies in the greater Yellowstone area for thirty-plus years, most intensively on the Madison.

Though not as continuously, I have fished the Madison for twenty-plus years and, during the mid-1980s, I guided out of West Yellowstone for four years. Many of my days with clients were spent on various rivers inside and outside Yellowstone Park—the Yellowstone, Gallatin, Firehole, Lamar, Gardner, and Slough Creek—but most of my days were spent floating various sections of the Madison River. It became not only a regular river for me but also a favorite one.

The joy of guiding, if you want to call it a joy, is that you can't pick when you want to go fishing. As a guide you are out on the river at different times of the day in all kinds of weather. Often you learn as much from the clients as they learn from you. They fish the river with the techniques and fly patterns that they brought with them from their home waters. As a guide you get to see what works and doesn't work on a river such as the Madison. Every day on the water is an education. Hundreds of days of guiding all sections of the Madison greatly expanded my experience—and that expanded my knowledge.

Making the audio tape together was tremendous fun because we understood what makes the Madison both easy and difficult. And we understood how to fish it when it is easy and when it is difficult. For me the enjoyment was enhanced by the tremendous depth of Craig Mathews' experience and knowledge, but more than that, it was really magnified by his great passion for the river. This man really loves the Madison.

The question and answer format of the two-day recording session, captured and presented in the acclaimed audio tape, *Fly Fishing the Madison*, is transformed and updated here into book form. It is presented in a single voice, Craig's, though, obviously, there were two voices and give and take recorded throughout the session.

There was also a third "voice" not actually heard in the audio tape—the voice calling suggestions from the other room, the voice making us go over a particular point two and three times until we got it right, and finally the voice that belonged to the hand and mind that cut and spliced the eight hours of raw tape into an easy-listening, ninety-minute format. That voice belonged to project editor Stan Bradshaw—he was our intellectual guide.

This book reads so well because it is such tight copy. The three of us: Craig, Stan, and I, created the audio version and it is because this written version started as an audio tape that it is such a fast-paced, information-packed book on the Madison.

The credit for really knowing the Madison goes to Craig. He was amazing. Often, during the taping session, I wanted to reach for pad and pencil to make notes while he was talking. Then, I would remember that I didn't have to write down his words, that everything was being recorded. Still, there were many moments when I wished that his ideas were down on paper. Now they are.

Finally, I learned more from Craig Mathews than just how to fish the Madison River—in listening to him, I learned a lot about fly fishing. So will you. And you will enjoy reading about a great trout river.

THE MADISON RIVER
FROM ENNIS TO THREE FORKS

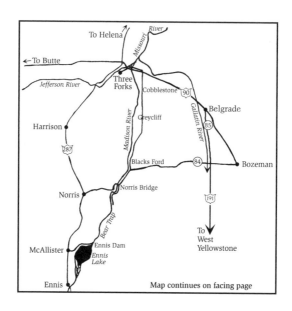

Map continues on facing page

CLOSED TO FISHING FROM BOATS
designated by shaded area

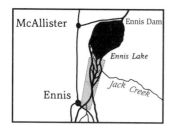

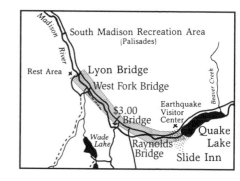

THE MADISON RIVER
FROM YELLOWSTONE PARK TO ENNIS LAKE

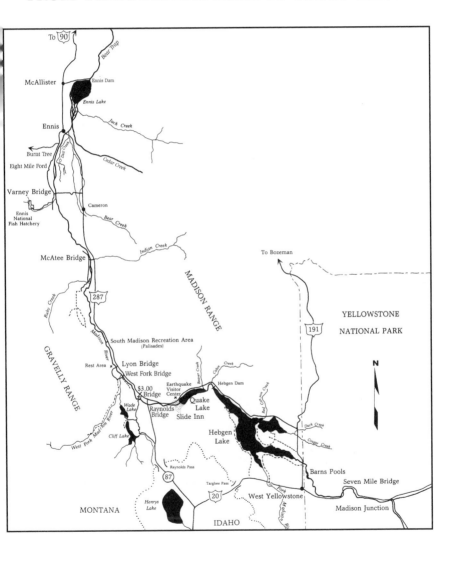

Madison River near Seven Mile Bridge in Yellowstone National Park

INTRODUCTION

Charles Brooks once told me that one cannot own a river, or even a part of it, except in one's heart. He knew the Madison River, it was in his heart and he loved it. The same goes for me. I fish the river over seventy days a year. But if I had to pick just one day to fish the Madison River I would go in June, just below Madison Junction in the Park. It would be a nasty day with wet snow. The bugs would be everywhere and I would fish dry flies through several Pale Morning Dun emergences.

The Madison is so famous that anglers tend to show up on the river with a lot of preconceived notions about how to fish it. They try to fish it as they fish their own home rivers—the same flies, the same techniques. Most will spend several days on the river and never get to experience the best of it.

One of the toughest ideas to grasp for most anglers new to the Madison is that the river has a lot of microhabitat and microdistribution—more than most other rivers. You can have a caddis emergence in one fifty-yard stretch of water and a mayfly spinner fall on the next fifty yards. You may do well fishing a spinner fall, only to come upon a caddis hatch around the next bend. You may be skunked if you don't recognize the change in hatch and adjust to it.

So a lot of experience may not prepare you to fish the Madison because it's unique. There are no "averages" you can trust about this river. Even though two pieces of water look alike, on closer examination they are quite different. To succeed, you must be adaptable.

1

Most first-time visitors to the Madison try to fish too much of the river in their short visits. They'll fish one spot for an hour or two then run somewhere else. I sympathize with the impulse to want to experience it all, but it can't be done. Those who try usually go home frustrated. So pick one section of river and get to know it.

Of course, a lot depends on when you're on the Madison. If you are here in June, concentrate your efforts on Yellowstone National Park. When the runoff starts, avoid the Park because of turbid water. Hebgen and Quake Lakes serve as silt traps and the river below these lakes stays clear longer into the spring.

Bring a reasonable expectation when you fish the Madison. I will never forget the phone call I had a few seasons back. While booking a week of guide trips with us, a fellow asked, "Geez, if I catch a large fish, could I get it mounted?" I replied that we encourage catch-and-release fishing but that there is a taxidermist in town. He said, "Yeah, I usually let most fish, you know, under 20 go, but if I catch a fish over 20, I'd like to have it mounted."

I replied, "Well you probably will catch a fish over 20 inches."

And he said, "No, I mean over 20 pounds." He expected to catch a trout over 20 pounds—they don't exist in the Madison River.

A 20-inch fish is a reasonable expectation, but people still tend to have inflated expectations about the numbers of 20-inch-plus fish they'll catch. People occasionally come expecting days full of them. While the 20-inchers are there, they tend to be elusive. And the likelihood of big fish depends on the time of year you are here. If you fish the Madison in the heat of summer, you might reasonably expect to catch a couple fish in the 20-inch class in a week's effort. But don't come expecting to see fish like that every day.

Often I'll have fly fishermen come into the shop and tell me that they've taken several fish over 24 inches. I know better.

On the other hand, if you fish in the Park in the early season when spawners are up from Hebgen Lake—not only the holdover brown trout from the previous fall, but the large spring-spawning rainbows—you can reasonably expect to catch some really large fish. The same holds true in the fall, when the fall spawners come out of Hebgen.

But the average fish on the Madison is smaller than the 20-inch benchmark. A typical day for an experienced angler on the Madison—with or without a guide—would be any-where from ten to twenty fish in the 10- to 18-inch category.

Madison River looking toward Madison Junction from the Seven Mile area in Yellowstone National Park.

CHAPTER 1

Sections of the River

MADISON JUNCTION TO SEVEN MILE BRIDGE

In June few people fish the Madison in the Park. It wasn't always this way. In 1994 Yellowstone Park introduced a fee permit for fishing the Park. Today there are far fewer anglers on many of the Park's rivers. The Park issued 218,000 free fishing permits in 1978. In 1998 the Park issued only 67,000 fee permits. In 1990, when the popularity of fly fishing reached its height, Park officials recorded over 400,000 angler-days in the Park. In 1999 that number had dropped to only 240,000 angler-days. And the Madison River only receives 8 percent of the yearly total. And yet the river here provides some of the finest early-season dry-fly fishing that I know.

Madison Junction downstream to Seven Mile Bridge has nearly seven miles of great trout water. The road follows the river all along this stretch, making access easy. The fishing, however, is seldom easy. According to Charlie Brooks in his *Trout and the Stream*, only 20 percent of those fishing this water catch fish. Success depends upon stealth and concentration. The river is a succession of deep runs and pools with plenty of undercut banks. The bottom is carpeted with lush weed growth that often reaches the surface, creating a complex mix of cross currents. You must control drag to fish this stretch successfully. Long leaders and tippets will help.

Weather is a huge factor. If you get cloudy, rainy, or snowy days you are going to get some great Pale Morning Dun (PMD), early Blue-Winged Olive (*Baetis*), and Gray Drake hatches. On warm evenings look for Grannom and Spotted Sedge. In early to mid-June expect Giant Golden and Little Yellow Stonefly emergences.

From mid-September to November Blue-Winged Olives emerge again. In the fall the river fills with pre-spawning browns and rainbows that run up from Hebgen Lake. These trout average 17 inches, with many fish over 20 inches, and feed on Blue-Winged Olive duns. Good patterns include size-20 to -22 *Baetis* and size-16 Pale Morning Dun nymphs and emergers; size-12 Gray Drake Sparkle Duns; and Pale Morning and Gray Drake Hackled Spinners. The best caddis patterns are the Deep Sparkle Pupa and Emergent Sparkle Pupa, the Antron Caddis Pupa, and size-14 and -16 Iris and X Caddis. Stonefly nymph patterns like the Brooks' Giant Stone, Kaufmann Golden Stone, Mathew's Nature Stone, and the Natural Drift Stonefly Nymph, in sizes 4 to 6, work best for the big stoneflies. A size-12 Little Yellow Stone Nymph works fine. To cover the adult phase of the stoneflies, use the Henry's Fork Salmon Fly, Flex-Stone, and Bullet Head Golden Stone in sizes 4 and 6, along with size-12 to -14 Stimulators to imitate the Little Yellow Stones.

From mid-July to mid-August, the river might be too warm for good angling. When water temperatures reach the high sixties the trout become lethargic and won't readily come to the fly. The Firehole River and the geysers increase water temperatures and the fish become snake-like from not feeding. They will often have huge heads, skinny bodies, and will barely offer resistance when hooked. Most larger trout will head downstream to Hebgen Lake to escape the heat. During high water temperatures, give the fish that stay in the river a break and fish somewhere else until the water cools.

In good water years, like we had in the late 1990s, the river remains cool all summer. In these years there are great hatches and the trout feed all summer. Check with one of the local fly shops for current water conditions if you are planning to fish the river in the heat of the summer.

Generally, in mid- to late August, the river cools down with the first early frosts. You can practically set your watch by it—August 20. As the river begins to cool, the fall Blue-Winged Olive, or *Baetis*, hatch begins, and the fish start to feed on the surface again. Terrestrials like ants, beetles, and grasshoppers will also bring the trout to the surface. From late summer into fall the hoppers fill the meadow stretches. When the hopper winds of August and September fill the water with the bugs, the trout throw caution to the wind. Put your hopper imitation within a foot of the bank, where trout are used to seeing grasshoppers. Use a short, 20- to 25-foot cast. This is exciting fishing and if the wind is blowing a gale and bringing naturals onto the water you can get into some huge trout on grasshopper flies.

The Madison in the Park has been referred to as the largest chalk stream in the world. It is rich in weeds and insect life. The weed beds in this stretch are important cover in the summer. In the early season, when the river is cool, trout are all over the river. As the water drops and warms, in late June, the larger trout move to the weed beds. From late June to mid-August, small trout are in the riffles, and large trout are

Downstream from Madison Junction, in the Elk Meadows area, the river offers prime dry-fly water that can be challenging to fish.

near the weed beds. In the fall, when the spawners from the lake enter this stretch, the large trout will be in the deeper runs and pools. These fish are used to the security of the lake's depths. When they run up into the river, shadows, movement, and sounds will spook them into areas of greater depth.

Downstream from Madison Junction, the river is a classic meadow stream. This is prime dry-fly water, with plenty of brown and rainbow trout along with mountain whitefish and the occasional grayling. But this is also tough fishing. While the surface appears smooth, the river's bottom is full of drop-offs, mounds, and weed banks. It is difficult to get a drag-free float. And you'll likely have the distraction of a wildlife show. Often there will be elk, bison, sandhill cranes, and Canada geese in the meadow, with the occasional grizzly or black bear.

A mile below Madison Junction is Big Bend. The river leaves the meadow, flows away from the road below National Park Mountain, and returns to the highway at the Elbow Pool and Deer Lick. This is productive water. The river narrows and quickens, and the bottom becomes channeled. You'll find Elbow Pool where the road comes closest to the river, a half mile below the western edge of the meadow. Deer Lick is less than one hundred yards downstream, at the next bend. There is a natural deer lick on the opposite bank here. Both these pools are excellent places to fish, first during the salmon fly hatch in June and again during the fall spawning run.

Both spots are tough to fish. Deer Lick gives anglers fits. People tend to wade out halfway across the river and cast to the opposite bank, where trout hold. Most cast their fly far into the backwater, with their line landing in the main current. The current immediately drags the fly away from the bank. Next they will wade further across and put their fly, leader, and line entirely in the backwater. Now everything sits in the backwater, giving the trout far too long to inspect their fly. The best approach is to cast to the seam where the backwater and main current merge.

Below Deer Lick are a couple of long riffles with lots of good trout at the right time of the year. It is seldom fished. During the Salmon Fly hatch in early June nice browns and rainbows rise to naturals. From mid-August until early November, many fall-run fish will hold behind the large submerged boulders in this stretch. Prospect with a large streamer or stonefly pattern.

A half mile above Mount Haynes, about three miles downstream from Madison Junction, there is more meadow water, known locally as Upper Haynes. Just above a large island there is a riffle with great holding water for spawning fish on the bank nearest the road. Your impulse may be to stand where you should be fishing. Trout hold on the road side of the riffle, just before it goes around the bend, at the head of the island. Approach this spot from either the near side, just below the parking lot, and stand well back from the shoreline, or wade to the opposite side and cast back to the holding water.

This meadow water is great dry-fly fishing. Undercut banks and deep water hold big trout. Salmon Flies, Gray Drakes, Pale Morning Duns, and a couple of caddis species bring trout to the surface in the early season. Tiny Blue-Winged Olives hatch all spring, but the water here is usually too deep in the early season for fish to feed on the emerging Blue-Winged Olives. In the fall, when the tiny Olives emerge again and the water is much lower, the trout will feed on the duns. I've watched anglers fishing the fall-run browns and rainbows with huge streamers ignore the tiny duns on the water, and the big trout rising to them. From noon to 4 p.m. these small mayflies can bring up large trout.

Below the island the river comes into the Mount Haynes area in a deep, slow bend. There is a parking lot and board-walk for handicapped access. This area holds some fine trout and whitefish all season.

Downstream the river turns a corner and comes back to the road in a two-hundred-yard run that ends at the Talus Story turnout, just upstream of Nine Mile Hole. This piece is studded with weed beds and channels. In the early season you can usually watch trout rising to PMDs or Gray Drakes if you drive by at the right time. Evening caddis emergences and egg-laying flights bring the fish to the surface. It's a popular spot, so if you fish here you can expect a crowd of onlookers when you hook a trout. At the Talus Story parking area the river is deep and fast. In the fall, spawning browns and rainbows often stop and rest here.

Don't be surprised if you attract as big a crowd as the wildlife. And don't forget to leave a wide safety zone between you and the bison, grizzlies, moose, and elk that may be sharing the river with you.

Swinging big Soft Hackles or stripping streamers is a great way to get vicious strikes out of these big fall-run trout. The rest of the season this stretch is seldom used by large trout. Small fish seem to enjoy the talus area all summer, as does a family of otters.

Nine Mile Hole is next. It has several large boulders in the river. The run ends where the river breaks around the bend a quarter mile below. These rocks fell off the north rim of the volcanic caldera that forms the northern edge of the Madison Canyon. They fell from the canyon wall into the river during frequent earthquakes. These boulders collect logs, weeds, and other debris, causing the river to flow in many directions. In places it is nearly impossible to get a drag-free drift here. Nine Mile Hole is home to some fine trout all season, and it serves as a holding spot during the fall run for hundreds of good trout. Patience is the key here. In the early season you can expect to see fish feeding on Salmon Flies, Golden Stones, and Little Yellow Stoneflies. Look for mayflies such as the Pale Morning Dun, and Gray and Green Drakes. Caddisflies, especially the Spotted Sedge and Little Sister Sedge, are always present in the evenings in late June, July, and mid-August.

Midway through the hole there's a small stream entering the river from the opposite bank. In the evening, when trout feed on emerging or egg-laying caddis, cross the river to reduce drag. At times there are a dozen or more good fish feeding on the surface here.

During the summer in good water years, when the fish stay in the river and don't move downstream to Hebgen, this is good grasshopper and cricket water. Around August 20 you might come upon a flying ant swarm along the river. These ant swarms can produce incredible rises of trout in the late morning and early afternoon.

In the fall, when the spawning fish are in the river, Nine Mile Hole draws anglers from all over the world. It holds many large trout all fall. Streamers, big stonefly nymphs, and Soft Hackles are effective. Fish begin to show up in September and their numbers continue to increase until the season closes in early November.

Fish this section slowly and carefully in the late season. I've had times when I've taken a trout on my first cast of the early morning. Then too, I've had a fish take on my tenth cast in the same run. Wade carefully and don't send waves into the middle of the river. Careless wading spooks the trout holding in the middle channel. Cast a short line after wading slowly into position rather than letting fly with a chuck-and-chance-it bomb that spooks trout used to the secure depths of the lake. Spawning trout are spooky.

Take care to fish even the shallow water near shore when you arrive in the mornings, especially if you have arrived before others have spooked the trout back into the depths of midriver. Large trout often patrol the shallows in search of sculpins, stonefly nymphs, and other food before the sun hits the water. On cloudy days with rain or snow the fish are less spooky and you might find them cruising the shallows all day long.

After Nine Mile Hole, the river comes up to the road and flows alongside it for nearly a quarter mile before turning south and heading back into a swampy area. This short stretch along the road is great dry-fly and nymph water. A few boulders and logjams create good holding water and perfect habitat for a few mayfly, caddisfly, and stonefly species. In June and early July you might come upon a good Pale Morning Dun or Gray Drake spinner fall from 8 a.m. to 11 a.m.

When you hook up you'll stop traffic. A few years ago a couple friends and I were fishing a PMD spinner fall on the morning of July 4. The traffic was heavy for the holiday and the three of us were all into fish at one point. A tour bus stopped to watch, then another, and then several cars stopped and several tourists got out with their cameras. A short time later a park ranger stopped and asked us to come into shore and show him our licenses. By the time we waded out there were nearly thirty people gathered around us. Expect a crowd here.

At the end of this stretch you will see a large island just where the river leaves the road and heads back into the swamp. From this point downstream for over a mile the river flows through what once was a nasty swamp. When Charlie Brooks referred to this stretch in the 1970s he said one should not pursue the trout too far into this "troublesome and dangerous area." Brooks neglected to mention that this was one of his favorite haunts to fish. It has changed since. In 1988, Yellowstone Park experienced severe fires in this area. The streamside lodgepoles and willows burned away. The beaver left the area, and the bogs along the river dried up as the beaver dams fell apart with no maintenance. The deep holes have filled in from silting after the fires. It took better than a decade after the fires for the area to begin to come back. Tiny aspens are appearing along with some willows. Good water years are beginning to flush out some of the silt, and logjams are being created again. It'll take several more years to return this area to what it once was for wild trout, but it is coming back. This is the only area along the river that was negatively affected by the fires of 1988. The stretch ends at Seven Mile Bridge.

Most of the fish you see rising near the swans are whitefish or very small trout. The area from the bridge upstream to the island just below Nine Mile Hole is open meadow and visible from the highway. This is a great place to view bison, grizzly and black bears, elk and moose, ospreys and bald eagles from your vehicle. A word of caution—avoid approaching any wildlife too closely anywhere in Yellowstone, especially here. I recently watched tourists walk out into the downfall near river's edge to photograph a moose. They nearly stepped on its calf as it lay hidden in the downfallen timbers, and the chase was on. The cow moose nearly outran these careless folks. If she had caught them she likely would have stomped them into the mud.

NOTE: The river upstream for one-half mile above Seven Mile Bridge is closed to angling due to nesting trumpeter swans. Please obey the signs and stay clear of the swans.

SEVEN MILE BRIDGE TO THE BARNS POOLS

The reach between Seven Mile Bridge downstream to the Barns Pools runs for nearly six miles. From Grasshopper Bank below the bridge to Riverside Drive you'll have good fishing with grasshopper, cricket, bee, beetle, and ant flies along the sagebrush bank from July to October.

This stretch of water is full of aquatic weeds that extend all the way to the surface in many places. Try and fish in the channels between the weeds rather than over the weed beds. If you hook fish they always seem to head for the weeds. It's nearly impossible to horse a good fish over weed banks.

At the head of Grasshopper Bank is a small island and a drive-through parking area. Fish usually rise here all summer during the morning hours between 9 a.m. and 11 a.m. Big, submerged rocks in this stretch can make for tricky wading, so watch your footing.

Just below the island the river comes up to the road and runs along it for over a half mile. We call this run Rip-Rap because of the boulders the Park Service placed to protect the road from erosion. The run is deep and fast and holds good fish in the fall in the upper two-thirds of its 300-yard length. During the rest of the season most fish hold in the lower third. In the fall it's usually best to fish this run from the road side. Downfall and standing timber can severely limit your backcast here and generally inhibit your ability to effectively fish this reach. This is a perfect situation for a spey rod.

Downstream of Rip Rap for the next few hundred yards the river is slow, mostly deep, and weedy. The hatches can be great in the early season. PMDs, Blue-Wing Olives, and Gray Drakes are around from early June to mid-July. Evening caddisfly activity can be fun, too, when *Brachycentrus* and *Hydropsyche* are on. The better trout feed on the opposite shore and are difficult to approach. The water against the far bank is shallow and slow moving, and the larger trout prefer to sip insects here rather than in midriver. There's an old eagle's nest on the roadside bank, now occupied by a pair of ospreys that continually harass the trout, making them skittish and even more aware of your approach.

This is on-your-knees fishing from the far side. I like to inch along on my knees or scoot on my hind end until I'm within a short 15- to 25-foot cast away. Then I try a pinpoint accurate upstream hook cast to keep the tippet off to one side of the fish. If you line these fish, you put them down.

At the upstream end of Riverside Drive the river loses its chalk-stream character and becomes freestone, riffle-type water. For the next few miles of river—from Riverside Drive downstream to the Cable Car Run and the Barns Pools—there isn't much holding water. The riffles run over lava rock, and there is not much insect life. Mostly it is pretty barren. It is also seldom over knee deep. If you can find a run—and there are a half dozen such runs in this five-mile stretch of river—you'll find some fish in it in the spring and fall, but generally they pass quickly through it. This stretch looks a lot better than it actually fishes. For the most part, leave it alone. If you want to spend a few years of early spring and fall fishing, you could probably locate a few spots along this stretch that hold fish.

There was an old park ranger named Shakey Beiley who fished this stretch religiously all spring and fall. He would take some really large brown trout. It took him several years to locate the little pockets and runs. And he probably knew each one of the fish by name. There just aren't that many of them in there. I know of six.

BARNS POOLS TO HEBGEN LAKE

One of the most popular sections on the Madison runs from the Barns Pools (aka "Barns Holes") downstream to Hebgen Lake. This section is nearly six miles of bends,

One of the most popular sections of the Madison runs from the Barns Pools, shown above, downstream to Hebgen Lake. Barns Pools are named for the barns that used to house the Park's horses and stagecoaches.

(Photo by Stan Bradshaw)

pools, islands, glides, and runs connected by short, fast pieces of water. A half mile inside Yellowstone's West Entrance is a dirt road on the north side of the main highway. It leads to the Barns Pools. These pools are named for the stables that used to house the Park's horses and stagecoaches. When you arrive at the end of the road you'll be at Hole #1. Upstream, just around the bend, is the Cable Car Run, and downstream around the bend are Holes #2 and #3.

For the next three miles downstream the river meanders northwest in a series of oxbows to the Park's western boundary. This part of the river is only accessible by hiking downstream from the Barns Pools or by hiking upstream from Baker's Hole Campground on the Montana state line. Locals refer to this stretch of water as Beaver Meadows because of the numerous beaver holes and lodges along the banks. This area is also a great place to see moose and bears.

As the river meanders through the meadow, undercut banks and deep pools provide wonderful security and holding water for the fish. While the Barns Pools are best known and get the most fishing pressure, there are other pools below in the Beaver Meadows that get little pressure and have excellent fishing. Much has been written about the Barns Pools, and many coming to this area spend their entire vacation fishing just the Barns Pools. If you fail to explore the miles of water below the pools you will miss out on some very good fishing.

I have seen twenty cars and more parked in the #1 and #2 Hole parking areas. Some anglers arrive well before dawn. Many anglers stand in line and wait their turns to fish through the holes, and rightfully so. These holes hold dozens of pre-spawning trout up from Hebgen Lake. The trout begin running up river the first week of August, with the big males the first to arrive. By late August a few females come in, but the strongest fall fishing is still weeks away, always after September 20. By the middle of October this area is packed with browns and fall-run rainbows.

This stretch is primarily a spring and fall fishery, with both brown and rainbow trout running up from Hebgen Lake. Most years, when the water starts to warm in mid-July, the fish head back downstream to the lake for the summer. On good water years however, trout remain in the river all summer, feeding on evening caddisfly emergences and terrestrial insects.

Fall fishing should focus on migrating trout prior to their spawning. It is unsportsmanlike to fish for trout that are actively spawning. So don't do it. In addition, it's destructive to the fishery. Studies show that anglers wading through spawning redds can destroy most of the eggs.

SPEY RODS ON THE MADISON

A fairly new way of fishing the Madison during spring and fall angling for run-up trout uses Spey rod techniques. This allows presentations in areas where trees and other obstructions make back casts impossible. Spey techniques give anglers a fixed-length presentation without false casting, allowing casts to fall into the same holding water each time. Flies plop in quick succession before the trout and in the right spot. These techniques are just now evolving and they will become a greater part of successful western angling.

When fall fish become territorial before spawning they become susceptible to streamer imitations. There has been much speculation as to what causes migrating trout to feed or to become territorial and slam streamers. No one knows for certain. Talk with any local angler and you'll hear anything from "its the weather" to "its the moon phase." I think that the level of aggression depends on the calendar—the later the better, and late October is always best.

When fall-run trout become territorial before spawning you can do better with floating lines and unweighted flies. Sinking lines catch on everything and are always tangled. Stick with floaters and add nonlead weight on your leader if you need it.

When fish are territorial I cast a bright, unweighted streamer on a tight line across and down, working the fly against the banks or in the deep pools and runs, then retrieve it with long, rapid strips. It's exciting to watch a trout come several feet to the surface to take a streamer.

This presentation works best late in the season, when the fish are looking for anything to hit. Overcast, snowy, or rainy conditions are best because the trout are less skittish under cloud cover.

When it's bright and clear and the trout are reluctant to move far, try a weighted streamer using the cast described in the last paragraph. But allow your fly to sink by mending once or twice. Then let it float dead-drift or use a very slow retrieve. When the fish takes, resist the impulse to set the hook. Instead, allow the trout to hook itself. Usually a fish taking a sculpin hits the fly first to shock or stun it and then returns to it immediately. If you do strike, you might pull the fly away from him.

Another good fall and spring tactic for fishing this area is to use steelhead tactics and flies like Babines, Glow Bugs, Marabou Single Eggs, Marabou Spawn Sacs, and Fly Fur Streamers that imitate rainbow and brown trout fry or eggs. Fish these patterns dead-drift, bouncing them right over the bottom and right past the nose of the target fish. Nothing works better at getting a reluctant spawner to strike than an egg or fry imitation. This type of fly triggers some instinctive urge in the fish—the trout grabs it even though it has no intention of eating it. These patterns are often the best choice early in the spawning run, before the trout become very aggressive.

Remember, these are the same trout that sip mayflies, caddisflies, and midges all spring and summer off the surface of the lake. They will take dries when they are in the river, and the earliest fall fish sip the Trico mayflies from 9 a.m. to noon throughout August and September. They also feed on the Blue-Winged Olives, beginning in September until the end of the fishing season in early November.

These fish also like huge grasshopper and cricket flies in the late summer and early fall. I like to fish flies like the

Lamar Cricket in sizes 4 and 6 along the banks and in the deep pools of the Beaver Meadows. On a recent late August afternoon, I cast one of these monstrosities and took several browns and two rainbows up to 19 inches, all run-up trout.

HEBGEN LAKE

Hebgen is like several different lakes wrapped up into one huge one. Completed in 1915, and named for the engineer who designed it, it's nearly sixteen miles long and three miles across at its widest point, and eighty feet deep at the dam. Grayling Arm, Madison Arm, and South Fork Arm all come together at the southern portion of the lake to form the main stem of Hebgen Lake itself down to Hebgen Dam.

Hebgen provides brood fish to naturally restock wild trout into streams like Grayling, Duck, the South Fork of the Madison, Trapper, and Watkins. A rich lake, it is famous for gulper fishing in spring, summer, and fall. Bud Lilly coined the term "gulpers" thirty years ago to describe the sound made when these large trout feed on the surface on midges, mayflies, and caddisflies.

In May, just after ice-out, the trout begin feeding on the huge Diptera that come off. There is no "best place" to find trout feeding on these midges. The prevailing winds come from the southwest, making the southern sections of the lake less windy.

Midges in the early season prefer bright, warm, calm weather. Every evening around seven o'clock, the wind drops and huge clouds of midges emerge off the lake. The earlier the lake calms, the earlier the hatch will come off. On warm spring mornings the activity can start by nine in the morning. It is totally wind and weather dependent.

Typically, I arrive at Hebgen around 7 p.m. and spend time searching from shore, usually with binoculars, to determine where the fish are rising strongest. This changes from

Hebgen Lake provides brood fish that naturally restock wild trout into its tributary streams. Anglers will find that it also offers a full range of lake fly-fishing action.

(Photo by Stan Bradshaw)

day to day. I'll then head out in my boat towards the risers, being careful not to cause waves on my approach. I will use a two-fly rig, with a crippled midge with a trailing shuck on the top and a pupa as the trailer on the bottom. It's important to use a crippled pattern because it floats in the film, where the trout are used to taking cripples and pupae. Never cast more than fifty feet to risers. If possible try to hold your cast to thirty feet. Be patient and try not to spook fish with a bad presentation.

Trout feeding on midges in Hebgen connect their rises in a rhythm in which they rise every few feet. We refer to this as tracking. Tracking fish are the ones that will most likely rise to a fly. Keep false casting to a minimum; trout will spook at your back cast, as well as at your forward cast. Usually on Hebgen when trout are working midges they will feed on them in pairs or packs of three to five fish.

You might see trout wheeling and circling in a small area as they rise to naturals. Competition becomes a factor as fish race each other to insects. This is one of the few times flock shooting works. Drop your imitation into the frenzy, fish it actively, and you should hook up.

On Hebgen a dead-drifted midge pupa or crippled adult is seldom effective. Midge pupae rest vertically in the surface film prior to emergence. They dive for the bottom when they "feel" the approach of a trout. Cast in front of a riser and draw your fly slowly and steadily across his path, imitating the behavior of the natural.

If all else fails, smack the rising trout on the head with your fly. I've seen the hatch of midges so strong that it seems trout either don't see or ignore my fly. That's when smacking them on the head may work.

When fishing midges, or any dry flies, on Hebgen Lake, pay attention to wind and currents on the lake that produce what local anglers refer to as scum lanes and slop troughs.

Scum lanes are areas where the current meets weed banks and forms lanes that collect insects in huge numbers along their edges. It is not unusual to have scum lanes on the main portion of Hebgen and the Madison Arm that run for over one hundred yards. Slop troughs are large, calm pieces of the lake that haven't yet been disturbed by late morning or afternoon winds.

Sometimes scum lanes and slop troughs come together to concentrate thousands of bugs. There might be dozens of trout rising, sounding like farm animals feeding in a barnyard. Usually around 2 p.m. the wind comes up and puts the whole dry-fly show to an end for the day. But, if the wind does start to blow early, around 10 or 11 a.m. don't be too quick to head to shore. Often the wind settles back down after a short time and the fish start feeding again.

Early season midges are enormous, by midge standards— sizes 12 to 16. Trout feed greedily on them, right at the edge of the early season's receding ice along the lake's shoreline. Fish cruise the ice flows in early May, picking off the first insects of the season.

These large midges provide great dry-fly challenges from early May well into June. You'll need both a pupa imitation and an impaired or crippled adult imitation. I like a size-14 Serendipity in gray, brown, or olive for the pupa. A size-14 to -16 Hebgen Midge or Griffith's Gnat Emerger works great for imitating the crippled adults

In mid-May you might come across early *Callibaetis* or Speckled Spinner hatches. The Madison Arm's south shoreline and southern section of the main lake are the best areas to find them. You find them in weed beds and mostly shallow, still water. The *Callibaetis* on Hebgen Lake are multibrooded so they appear again between late July and September. Late summer populations are the offspring of early summer broods.

Callibaetis emerge on the lake in the late morning and early afternoon, from about 10 a.m. to 2 p.m. Spinner falls usually coincide with the emergence. Around 10 a.m. you'll see aggressive rises as the trout chase the nymphs. Cast a size-16 *Callibaetis* Nymph to risers or around weed beds. Retrieve your nymph in short, quick strips. As the hatch gears up and more duns appear on the surface, trout begin to link rise forms every few feet, feeding on the duns. This is gulping at its best. Single out a fish and track its direction of travel, making sure he will pass within casting range. Pay close attention to weed beds and weed walls. An approaching gulper might run into a wall of weeds and then change direction, heading back the way he came, or he might travel with the weed wall, always parallel, never penetrating the weeds.

My favorite pattern for the dun is a *Callibaetis* Sparkle Dun or Cripple in size 16. The spinner is also a size 16. I like a *Callibaetis* Foam or Hackle Fiber Spinner. Usually trout don't show a preference when both duns and spinners are on the water. Since the spinner fall and emergence usually coincide, I stick with a dun pattern until late in the game. Then, when only spent mayflies are on the water, the fish sometimes prefer the spinner.

There are two tips to keep in mind when fishing the gulpers on Hebgen Lake. First, it's important to lead the fish enough with your cast so you can slowly pull on your line to remove any slack in your tippet. This will force your fly to come around and face your position. If you fail to do this, your fly might drag, even though you are fishing on "still" water. You can't detect the drag, but the trout will, and they'll refuse your fly.

Second, when the fish rises to your fly do not set the hook. When it comes to your fly, simply raise your rod and let go of the line. The weight of the line will be enough to set the hook. If you hang on to the line with your free hand the fish will break your tippet.

Hebgen's famed Trico emergence begins around June 20. This small mayfly has a few peculiar emergence and mating characteristics. The tiny males emerge at night and seldom offer fishing opportunities until the next morning. On Madison Arm the larger female duns emerge as early as 6 a.m. to 9 a.m. These morning emergences and spinner falls can provide wonderful dry-fly action.

Unlike the *Callibaetis*, Tricos emerge in the middle of the Arm, well out from the shoreline and away from the weed beds. The nymphs of the Trico are not worth imitating. Focus instead on the duns and spinners. I like a size-18 or -20 olive- or black-bodied Trico Sparkle Dun and a size-20 black Trico Spinner.

In late July and August flying ant activity on Hebgen can bring on big rises of trout. These insects fool everyone for awhile when they first arrive. When you see the aggressive rises to these insects, you may think the fish are taking *Callibaetis*, since the *Callibaetis* are emerging or spent on the surface. After several casts and no takers on *Callibaetis* patterns, take a cue from the ants that are swarming all over your boat, on your shirt, and in your face, and change to a flying ant imitation. A size-12 to -16 Flying Foam Ant in black or red will work.

In July and August you can arrive on the Madison Arm at 8 p.m. with time to spare if you want to fish the evening caddisfly activity. From eight to eleven o'clock trout aggressively rise to caddisfly emergences on the Arm. You will be all alone. Few anglers fish this hatch.

A size-14 to -16 tan Emergent Sparkle Pupa, or an X Caddis in the same size and color, are the only flies you need to fool these trout. It is usually best to skitter or drag these flies on the surface. Slowly lift your rod and strip one-foot sections of line. Do this three or four times and then let the fly sit for a few seconds. Use 4X tippet or you'll just be tying or buying more flies.

When you break off one of Hebgen's brutes, and you are sitting in your boat trying to tie on a new fly, make a pact with yourself not to look up, because you'll start shaking badly when you see all those fish feeding. When you are sitting there, tying on a new fly, you can look two feet away and there's some huge rainbow or brown trout looking you in the eye. Try to ignore these feeding fish when tying on a new fly.

Most anglers don't think about streamer or nymph fishing in Hebgen Lake, but from the time the ice goes off in May to freeze-up around Thanksgiving Day, streamers, leeches, mice patterns, and a variety of nymphs are responsible for huge catches of large trout. If you fish Hebgen when the ice goes off you can expect several days of great streamer action. You can follow the ice as it goes off the lake. Cast streamers onto the ice, let them slide off into the water, then begin a slow, steady retrieve. It's important to be where the ice is coming off. The fish seem hungrier and more aggressive as the ice melts away.

I tie streamers to imitate whitefish and Utah chub juveniles, which big brown trout in the lake like to eat. Years ago, I started tying these flies commercially, but most customers thought these patterns were meant for catching whitefish and chubs. So now we call them Fly Fur Streamers, after the material they are tied with, and sell them to the few anglers that spend serious time on the lake fishing streamers. They catch huge trout.

If you are a die-hard streamer fisherman you can fish a streamer in the middle of gulping trout and have real success. And some anglers will fish strictly nymphs. I know several elderly people who can no longer see a size-18 dry fly on the water. I used to feel sorry for these anglers until I watched them one day. They fish small nymphs and streamers and probably catch as many trout as anyone else does on dries.

I also know of those that fish the lake at night, with mice and huge saltwater-like streamers. Recently, one of them took a brown of over nine pounds. These hearty souls hit the water around 11 p.m. and head to coves like Moonlight and Trapper, and to spring creek inlets. They like dark nights, with little or no moon. One fishes a streamer on, or just under, the surface. Another pitches a hair mouse along the shoreline and retrieves in a "fast run on the surface." The mouser insists that you must retrieve your fly as if it is running back to shore, and not to the middle of the lake where a mouse wouldn't be heading. My question to this angler is, "Why would a mouse leave the shore anyway?" No matter what, some huge trout patrol the shoreline looking for mice, or whatever makes its way into the lake at night.

Good streamers for the lake include Fly Fur Streamers, sizes 2 to 6, Woolhead Streamers in olive and brown, sizes 2 to 6, and black and olive Woolly Buggers or Rubber Leg Buggers, sizes 2 to 8. Nymph patterns should include *Callibaetis* Nymphs, size 16, Olive Lake Scuds, sizes 12 to 14, Damsel and Dragon Fly nymphs sizes 10 to 12, and Evening Stars and Sparrow Nymphs sizes 10 to 12. If you care to fish the night away have a size-4 Hair Mouse and some 2/0 Red and White Deceivers.

While the Madison River Arm is the best known part of the lake, other areas offer some excellent prospects. The South Arm, formed by the South Fork of the Madison River, gets a good early-season emergence of *Callibaetis* in late May and June. The South Arm also is a staging area for spring rainbows and fall browns and rainbows that travel up the South Fork to spawn. It also gets good Pale Morning Dun and Green Drake hatches in July.

The Grayling Arm, formed by Grayling and Duck Creeks entering the lake, is a good place for Tricos and *Callibaetis* activity from June through September. All along the southern shoreline, from the South Arm to Hebgen Dam, a distance of over sixteen miles, expect to find fine midge and *Callibaetis* fishing. The south shore is also great for streamers and nymphs in and around the Rumbaugh-Spring Creek area. Rumbaugh Point and Bay always has the largest brown trout in the Montana Department of Fish, Wildlife, and Park's sampling nets.

One other point to remember when fishing here—at the height of the emergences you're going to see lots of rising fish. All those risers may not be trout. You are likely to find trout rising among whitefish or chubs. So if you stop and fish the risers and immediately take a chub or whitefish, don't assume that everything rising is a chub or whitefish. You have to be able to distinguish not only rise forms of the whitefish from the trout, but also the chubs from the trout. You can spend weeks fishing to the little splashy rise of a chub in the main body of the lake only to be disappointed, never hooking a trout because you spent all your time fishing to the chub rise.

For the most part, a chub has a splashy rise form. Look for the classic head and tail rise of the trout. You'll see the tip of the nose, then the dorsal fin, and finally the back fin. Head and tail rises mean that the fish are definitely trout. Whitefish will almost kiss the water. You will hear the sucking sound as they take in a fly, and then they'll flip their tails as they go downward. If you spend a few minutes and study the rise forms, you will be able to separate the trout from the whitefish and chub.

A few years ago all one saw on Hebgen Lake were float tubers. Today we see mostly pontoon-type kick boats, canoes, and whalers with casting platforms. There's still a few tubers around but the other watercraft get anglers to the fish quicker and more efficiently. If you use a float tube always keep an eye on the wind. Many times we have seen tubers blown across the Madison Arm or other parts of the lake, and then they had to make the long walk back to their vehicles, lugging their float tube with them. As with any large body of water, you have to be aware of sudden wind, lightening, hail, or thunderstorms. Be alert, take precautions, wear your life preserver, have a great time.

HEBGEN LAKE TO QUAKE LAKE

Hebgen Dam to the upper end of Quake Lake measures about one and a half miles, and the fishing season is open all year. This stretch, with large boulders and deep runs, holds some of the largest fish in the Madison River. The pools just below the dam hold huge trout. Anglers that fish these big, deep, noisy, swirling holes dredge up a few large trout. The water just below the dam is best from late October into November, when huge brown trout migrate up from Quake Lake either to spawn, or to feed on smaller members of the spawning run. All year the water coming out of the dam stays clear for the first half mile, until Cabin Creek enters and dumps its turbid snowmelt in late spring. During runoff this short piece of river gets plenty of pressure.

When the water is clear, I prefer the lower area, from Campfire Lodge downstream one mile to where it dumps into Quake Lake. Access is easy—take a left off Highway 287 at the Campfire Lodge turnoff a half mile downstream from the dam. Take the first right and follow the dirt road along the river for a mile, parking at a Forest Service gate. The gate protects critical bald eagle and osprey nesting sites. There are a few places to cross the river along the way, but for most of the year even the strongest waders cannot manage it. Of course, the fishing always seems better on the other side. Here it just may be so, where there are many great holding places and a side channel on the opposite side of the river.

From February to June, the river is packed with spawning rainbows. Nymphs will be your best bet—Beadhead Princes, Pheasant Tails, Glow Bugs, Serendipities, and large stonefly nymphs. But be prepared for midge and Blue-Winged Olive hatches that can bring the trout to the surface.

A Skwala stonefly might show up in the odd year and cause a rise. This stonefly lacks formed wings so it crawls around the snow banks, boulders, and logs along the shoreline, searching for a mate. A few tumble into the water, becoming available to trout. Sometimes in March and early April a size-10 to -12 Stimulator is effective for searching the shoreline and pockets above Quake Lake.

In May and early June, if runoff hasn't begun, this area has one of the most predictable emergences of early season *Baetis* anywhere. The best fishing is near the lake, where the river slows down and the trout can sip the emergers and duns easier than in the deep, fast water just upstream.

This stretch is one of few places on the river that gets a good Green Drake emergence in early July, about the same time that the Salmon Fly and Golden Stone hatches happen. Both the big drakes and the stoneflies always bring up good fish. These emergences are short-lived, so it's tough to plan on fishing any of them, but if you are on the Madison in early July, it can be worth checking out.

Evening caddisflies start to show as soon as runoff subsides. By early July, the river clears below its confluence with Cabin Creek and the evening caddisflies appear. From now through September caddisflies such as the Spotted Sedge, Short-Horn Sedge, Little Plain Brown Sedge, Great Gray Spotted Sedge, and a couple Green Sedge species bring on fine rises of trout.

There's about one and a half miles of pools, runs, and riffles between Hebgen Dam and Quake Lake and the fishing season is open all year. Anglers occasionally fool large trout in this section.

(Photo by Stan Bradshaw)

Summer terrestrial fishing is always effective here. Grasshopper, beetle, flying ant, bee, and cricket imitations will all bring up good fish in August and September.

But, day in and day out, big nymphs and streamers will be most effective. When no insects are pulling trout to the surface, and I want a chance to take some big fish, I'll go with nymphs and streamers.

Work upstream when fishing nymphs and streamers here. If you're fishing a large stonefly nymph, fish it dead-drift, using a short, heavy leader and tippet. If I'm fishing streamers in this kind of water I usually approach from the downstream, short-line-cast position, just as with the nymph.

A word of caution when fishing this area. Grizzly bears live here, as do mountain lions and moose. Once, as I fished just upstream of Cabin Creek, I watched from the river as a young grizzly digging ground squirrels just off the main highway stopped traffic near the Cabin Creek Campground. Tourists began wandering toward the bear with only video cameras and their illusions to protect them, all within sight of the river. Then a lady with a small frou-frou dog on a bright pink leash approached too closely. The little boar false charged, and the lady dropped her camera like a hot potato and ran, screaming and towing her choking, petrified pooch back to her Lincoln. It seemed quite funny at the time, but it could have ended with someone getting hurt. There are big animals in this country, and they are wild and dangerous.

QUAKE LAKE
THE GHOST OF AN EARTHQUAKE

Just before midnight on August 17, 1959, a huge earthquake caused a 7,600-foot-high mountain to slide, sending eighty million tons of earth and rock across the Madison River. This slide buried the Rock Creek Campground, where nineteen people were presumed to be covered by the tons of rock and dirt. Another seven were known dead. Things could have been much worse—there were dozens of other campers there that night. Estimates put the speed of the slide at nearly two hundred miles per hour as it fell into the Madison River Canyon. A tremendous gust of compressed air burst out from beneath the slide, throwing people, trailers, tents, and two-ton vehicles out of the slide path or the death toll would have been much higher.

Quake Lake, formed by the slide, is about twenty miles northwest of West Yellowstone. Its depth has decreased from nearly 250 feet to less than 180 feet. Each spring snowmelt cuts away at the spillway, lowering the lake's level. The size of the slide that created the lake is hard to fathom. Hoover

Dam, 726 feet high, contains only one-tenth of the material the Madison slide does.

Many old-timers still complain about the loss of five miles of the finest wild trout water in the world. Charlie Brooks told of rainbows averaging four pounds, with some weighing up to eight. He felt that the lake was "ugly" and the angling hazardous because of the dead timber left standing in the lake.

Quake Lake has the same insect emergences and requires the same fly patterns as Hebgen Lake does, although the Trico hatches on Quake Lake aren't as prolific as they are on Hebgen. It's eerie to fish among the dead trees and aquatic vegetation that grows on Quake. It's much like bass fishing in the South. There are dead trees, moss, and aquatic grasses. You won't find bass though. But you are likely to find chubs and some huge trout. The rise forms in the trees are mostly from the lake's healthy population of Utah Chubs. Trout will feed along the trees and you can recognize them by their classic head-and-tail rise. Chubs and whitefish always throw a bit of water when they take naturals, so be alert to rises and only fish for trout.

A good big-fish method on Quake is to work huge leech patterns along the stumps, dead timber, and rock slides. The challenge is similar to bass fishing—once you hook a good-sized brown trout it will head for the cover of the dead timber. You have to lean on him and try to move him out of the timber. I like to get to the other side of the obstructions, into the old river channel and open water, and fish back into the stumps and timber. If you hook a fish from here you can usually pressure him out of the trees and into the old channel.

Some of best fishing on Quake is with dry flies when the wind drops. The lower end of the lake, below Eagle Creek, is better during caddisfly times. The upper end usually has stronger mayfly activity. Be careful when boating near the bottom of Quake Lake. The current is strong as it leaves the lake

Eerie sentinels stand witness to the natural disaster that formed Quake Lake on August 17, 1959. The earthquake-caused slide that dammed the river killed twenty-six campers and created a lake where five miles of river previously flowed. Fish the old river channel or throw a leech pattern among the dead timber and stumps.   (Photo by Stan Bradshaw)

and you must pay attention so you don't get sucked down into the river below the lake.

The ice goes off Quake about ten days earlier than Hebgen Lake, around May 1. Unlike Hebgen, Quake's ice comes off quickly, in a day or two, where Hebgen's might take a week or longer. In the early season, if nothing is hatching in the upper lake, I like to fish the lower lake near where it dumps into the gorge. The fish cruise along the last little shelf of ice near the dead timber below the Earthquake Area Visitor Center. Use a size-4 to -6 Fly Fur Streamer or Woolhead Streamer in natural or olive to imitate chubs or rainbow trout fry. Cast the fly onto the ice, jerk it off, and strip it slowly. Beadhead Leeches work here too, in sizes 6 to 12, olive or black.

Other times, when no trout are feeding on the surface, fish a size-8 to -10 Sparrow or Evening Star Nymph. Work the area around the old riverbed, where most trout congregate in the early season. The old riverbed is easy to find. Get in your boat and head out beyond the dead timber until you move with the current. There's still a good current throughout the entire lake and not only will you feel the movement, but if you are in a float tube you'll notice a drop in water temperature. Once you find the current, hunt for pockets of debris such as vegetation and wood in little backwaters. The biggest fish in the lake feed in these backwaters. There are many huge trout in Quake Lake and it is virtually unfished when compared to the rest of the river.

In the early season Quake Lake has wonderful emergences of Blue-Winged Olives. The hatch is best on the upper lake, above the mouth of Beaver Creek, and occurs from about 10 a.m. to 4 p.m. The hatch is always better on overcast or rainy days. If the water is running clear the trout will feed on the duns from late April through May. Turbidity from Cabin Creek can sometimes shut this hatch down. For the early *Baetis* have *Baetis* Sparkle Duns, Cripples, Knocked Down Duns, and Diving Blue-Winged Olive Egg-Layers in sizes 18 to 22.

In June and July look for the Pale Morning Duns. The PMDs always come off best on the upper lake, above the mouth of Beaver Creek. You may occasionally need spinner imitations in the evenings, but the most consistent action will be on duns from 10 a.m. to 1 p.m. The evening spinner fall occurs about the same time as the caddisfly emergence, and the fish always feed on caddis better than on PMD spinners. For fishing the PMD hatch, use PMD Emergers and Sparkle and Crippled Duns in size 16. To imitate the spinners, fish a PMD Hackle Fiber Spinner in size 16.

Little Yellow Stoneflies bring up good risers on Quake Lake in July and August. At times fish will be up all over the lake feeding on these stoneflies. The action is best below the boat launch off Highway 287. When trout are taking Little Yellow Stoneflies, use a size-14 Little Yellow Stonefly or Yellow Stimulator. You may see larger fish taking caddisflies at the same time, so a size-14 tan X Caddis will do double duty, imitating both the caddis and the Little Yellow Stonefly. Most of the stonefly activity occurs from late afternoon into the evening.

Grasshoppers bring trout up on Quake while they don't on Hebgen. Along Quake's eastern shoreline, from the upper boat launch to Beaver Creek and along some of the shoreline opposite the highway, you can do well with grasshoppers in July, August, and September. Almost any hopper pattern will work here. I prefer a size-10 to -12 Chaos or Dave's Hopper.

I co-authored an article with John Juracek about Quake Lake for a national fly-fishing publication, trying to get some interest in fishing this wonderful lake. The article came out several years ago, but fishing pressure is still light.

More would fish it though, if they saw the photograph of the 31-plus-inch brown trout that came from Quake.

SLIDE INN

The Slide Inn or Slide section marks the start of forty miles of some of the finest trout water anywhere. This fishing exists largely because of the efforts of longtime Madison angler and guide, Dick McGuire, who almost single-handedly introduced the idea of wild-trout management to the Madison. His efforts, supported by the research of state biologists, led to the Montana Department of Fish, Wildlife, and Parks to cease the planting of catchable-size, hatchery-raised fish, first in the Madison, and eventually statewide. The stretch from Slide Inn down for many miles encompasses the part of the river on which the Department conducted its research.

The Slide Inn stretch of the river is some of the best wild trout habitat on the entire river. It's open to angling from the third Saturday in May through the last day of February.

The stretch from Quake Lake to Slide Inn—about one mile of river—is always in an uproar. We call this piece "The Gorge." The water is intimidating, noisy, heavy, boulder strewn, almost impossible to wade, and dangerous to approach. If you're going to fish the Gorge don't wade it. Have you ever seen the warning on television, "Don't try this at home," and wondered about the fool on the screen? People do wade Slide Inn. They march right across the seemingly impassable churning white water. But those people know the area intimately; and if you try to follow them, you just might drown. Stay safely on the edge when you are fishing at Slide Inn.

The ground is still unstable and rocks continue to fall from the canyon walls in this area more than forty years after the earthquake. When you look at this water from the highway all you see is solid white foam. When you stop and look more closely at it you'll note a little greenish-blue ribbon three or four feet wide on both sides of the river. This is where trout line up, waiting for food to pass by while avoiding heavy flows.

This reach used to have seeps issuing from boulder-lined banks, forming miniature spring creeks and numerous side channels in the lower end of the Gorge. These seeps and channels are mostly gone, having been filled in during the high-water spring flows of the mid-1980s. They were the most fun to fish from December to the end of February, just before the rainbows spawned here, during midge emergences. They will be back, nature will see to it. And when they return they'll be full of trout again. Please do not molest spawning trout in the seeps and channels when they return.

When opening day of the general Montana fishing season arrives in mid-May, this section of river is low and clear. PP&L controls the flow from Hebgen Dam, and in the early season flows from the dam are reduced to allow the capture of snowmelt in Hebgen Lake. Use a big (size-4) stonefly nymph, maybe a Brooks' Stone, a size-6 olive Cranefly Larva, a size-16 regular or Beadhead Krystal Serendipity in pearl or red, a Pheasant Tail, or a Woolhead Streamer around opening day.

Trail the Serendipity behind a stone nymph or weight it with a bead or split shot. The pearl-colored one usually takes more browns and the red takes mostly rainbow trout.

June runoff usually knocks out the fishing. Its power is intimidating. Huge boulders the size of Volkswagens move downstream as if they were pebbles. It's hard to imagine fish surviving the torrent.

By the end of June—almost never later than the 4th of July—spring runoff ends and the river becomes fishable. The first insects to bring the trout to the surface will be the caddisflies: Spotted Sedge (*Hydropsyche*), Short-Horn Sedge (*Glossosoma*), Great Gray Spotted Sedge (*Arctopsyche*), and

The Madison roars through a gorge below Quake Lake for about a mile. Almost impossible to wade and dangerous to approach, take extra care when fishing this reach. Or skip it altogether.

Green Sedge (*Rhyacophila*). All of them emerge about the time the river clears. You will need Deep Sparkle and Emergent Sparkle Pupa imitations, and Iris, X, and Spent Caddis patterns. The Salmon Fly, Golden Stone, and sometimes the Little Yellow Stonefly emergences show up then, too.

The water downstream to Slide Inn is mostly too fast and deep for mayflies. Occasionally you'll see Green Drakes, Small Western Green Drakes (Flavs), or Pale Morning Duns, but for the most part mayflies aren't significant here.

From mid-July to the end of September terrestrials like grasshoppers, crickets, big beetles, bees, and moths attract big trout. Pay special attention to the greenish-blue edge of water along the bank. In midsummer work the water with terrestrial imitations and attractor patterns such as big size-8 to -10 Wulffs, Trudes, Double Wings, and Stimulators. You'll lose many flies to big trout in this heavy, rough-and-tumble water even with a 3X tippet. The larger trout will usually hit in the deeper, faster water and head downstream like locomotives. You may well have to jog after them to have any chance of landing them.

SLIDE INN TO LYON BRIDGE

This is the favorite section of most anglers coming to fish the Madison. Access points like Raynolds Pass and Cliff-Wade Lake Bridge (locally known as the $3.00 Bridge because you have to pay three bucks in a streamside safe to fish from this private land), Big Bend, Pine Butte, Babbling Brook, and the West Fork are all well-known to anglers fishing this stretch. You can only wade fish in this section; float fishing is illegal. The fishing season is open from the third Saturday in May through February. This stretch is nine river miles long and is full of large boulders, slicks, hundreds of productive pockets, a few channels. It also has the most wild trout and mountain whitefish per mile of the entire river. The browns and rainbows average nearly 15 inches. Most anglers catch the more numerous rainbows.

At the lower end of this section, a mile upstream of the Lyon Bridge, is the West Fork of the Madison River. During spring runoff the West Fork dumps mud into the river. This clouds the river below the confluence, at times making it unfishable. If you plan to fish the river below here from late May to July 4, call ahead and check the water conditions.

The resident trout have changed their holding and resting water in the past ten years. When we did the Madison River audio tape in 1986, I explained that fly fishers should approach the Madison River as they would a little stream. I told anglers to look upon the river as if it was only five to ten yards wide. The great majority of good trout were bank fish. And I said to fish the banks and out from them for a

This typical Madison brown trout was caught near $3.00 Bridge in the Slide Inn to Lyon Bridge section that is open to wade-fishing only. No fishing from boats allowed here.

couple feet, as this is where all the trout would be. Today, all that has changed.

When the angling pressure increased and peaked in the early 1990s, the trout headed out from the banks for the protection of the heavier, deeper flows. Today, even though fishing pressure has decreased the last few years, the trout haven't returned to their old bankside holds. It's now more productive to get out to the boulders, slicks, seams, and pockets well off the banks.

In July and August, during evening caddisfly activity, you'll first see 5-inch to 7-inch trout surface feeding around 7 p.m. When you see this commotion, find a likely looking boulder with a nice slick behind it, or a quiet, shallow run a foot or two deep adjacent to heavier, deeper water. Now sit on the bank and watch the water for feeding fish. Usually by 8 o'clock you'll see a few larger trout begin to feed. These fish might be 12 inches and are most often rainbows. Now tie on a size-14 to -16 Emergent Sparkle Pupa in gold, amber, or olive or a size-14 to -16 Iris Caddis Emerger in the same colors. These patterns will produce where a standard Elk Hair Caddis would fail. By 9 p.m. larger trout begin to rise. When these bigger trout begin to feed, the little trout quit feeding. The larger trout have now moved in from the heavy water and they take over the prime feeding lanes in the last hour of daylight. Now put on a size-14 to -16 tan or olive X Caddis and fish it the rest of the night.

Too often during caddisfly time in July and August anglers come into the shop around dark, which is 10 p.m., and remark: "The fishing wasn't very good tonight." Or they show up in the morning complaining that the fishing never got going the night before, telling of leaving the river at 9 p.m. to come into town and have dinner. The secret is to stay until 9:30 or 10 p.m. for the chance to land the biggest trout of your trip.

Important caddisflies on this section of the river include: Spotted Sedge (*Hydropsyche*), Short-Horn Sedge (*Glossosoma*), Long-Horn Sedge (*Oecetis*), Little Plain Brown Sedge (*Lepidostoma*), Great Gray Spotted Sedge (*Arctopsyche*), and Green Sedge (*Rhyacophila*). Use flies such as the Emergent Sparkle Pupa and the Antron Caddis Pupa in brown and olive, sizes 14 to 16, the Iris and X Caddis, sizes 14 to 16. And egg-laying imitations such as LaFontaine's Diving Caddis are productive. But to be successful, you'll also need important fishing techniques and strategies. (See Chapter 4 for more information.)

Mayflies, such as the Blue-Winged Olive (*Baetis*), Western March Brown (*Rhithrogena*), Pale Morning Dun (*Ephemerella*), Small Western Green Drake or Flav (*Drunella flavilinea*), Pink Lady or Slate Cream Dun (*Epeorus*), and Green Drake (*Drunella grandis*), all emerge in good numbers and bring on big rises of trout. Nymph, emerger, dun, and spinner patterns are all important.

This stretch has phenomenal winter midge fishing. While I don't recommend contacting your travel agent to arrange a midwinter midge fishing trip here, if you do come to the area to ski or tour Yellowstone in the winter, bring your fishing gear. If the weather is right—and it often is in February—you can have some great dry-fly fishing. The only fly patterns you will need to fish the winter midge activity are pearl and red Krystal Serendipities in size 16, size-18 to -22 Griffith's Gnat Emergers, and size-16 to -22 Griffith's Gnats.

Stoneflies also emerge in good numbers all along this reach. The Salmon Fly comes in early July, Golden Stones closely follow, and Little Yellow Stoneflies are always on the water in July and August. Favorite nymphs include size-4 to -6 Brooks', Nature, and Natural Drift Stonefly Nymphs, size-6 to -8 Golden Stone Nymphs, and size-12 Little Yellow Stonefly Nymphs. Adult patterns should include the Henry's

Fork Salmon Flies, Flex-Stones, and Sunken Stones in sizes 4 to 6, for both the Salmon Fly and Golden Stone hatches.

Terrestrial fishing is good here too. Ants and beetles furnish the best terrestrial activity year in and out. Grasshoppers and crickets sometimes work well, but they seem to work better on the lower sections of the river. Carry some size-12 to -14 Chaos and size-12 to -16 Dave's Hoppers, black and red Foam or Fur Ants, and size-12 X Crickets. Terrestrials are best from mid-July through October, although I have taken trout on size-12 to -18 Black Foam Beetles all year long.

Flying ant swarms hit this part of the river around mid-August every year and big trout relish the naturals. I'll never be on the Madison without size-14 to -18 flying and regular ants in red, black, and cinnamon. When the insects splatter the surface, and the feeding frenzy begins, don't waste any time—the bonanza isn't going to last long and you have to cast quickly and accurately to individual, rising fish. In these situations don't "flock shoot," throwing casts in the middle of bunches of feeding trout.

Make sure you have a good selection of standard nymphs, such as size-8 to -14 Beadhead Princes, size-14 to -22 Pheasant Tails, size-14 olive, green, and brown Serendipities, size-14 R.A.M. Caddis, and size-12 to -14 Deep Sparkle Pupae in olive, tan, and bright green.

Individuals and groups such as the River Network, Montana Land Reliance, Trust for Public Lands, Trout Unlimited and Artemis are working hard to prevent wild trout habitat destruction along the Madison River, and on this stretch in particular. These groups are attempting to preserve over three miles of the nine total miles of river. In Appendix 4 there is a list of organizations striving to preserve what is left of this last best place of wild trout fishing in the United States. Please support these groups.

From Lyon Bridge downstream for more than thirty highway miles, the river is open to float fishing. Many anglers mostly use their boats for transportation from one good wade-fishing spot to the next.

LYON BRIDGE TO MCATEE BRIDGE

Lyon Bridge is about a mile below the West Fork of the Madison River. From here downstream for over thirty highway miles the river is open to fishing from boats. The first half of this open-to-float-fishing water is the Lyon to McAtee stretch. At casual glance, the river looks much the same. Many anglers call the entire section the "long riffle."

Often sections within this stretch are identified by the tributary creeks. You'll hear a section called Snowball or Wolf or Squaw or Papoose. Remember these names because you might be directed to fish one of these sections by reference to the tributary. Perhaps more importantly, you can find excellent dry-fly fishing around the mouths of these feeder streams.

This is a difficult section to learn without a guide. First, you have to cover a lot of water. Second, the water looks easy to fish, but there are several long stretches that are too shallow to provide security for large trout.

I like to float this area using the boat only for transportation. On arriving at good holding water, we'll get out of the boat and wade fish.

Fishing from a boat is a different game altogether. You move fast and you have to respond quickly. Spend too much time false casting and you'll lose chances at prime spots. Learn to finish one drift with your fly while glancing quickly downstream to pick out the next target ahead of the boat, and then throw a quick, slack-line quartering cast. You do this hundreds of times during the day, often relying on peripheral vision to spot rising trout or good-looking water ahead of you.

When you fish with a guide, listen to him. The guide can act as your eyes and will inform you of upcoming boulders, holding areas, seams, slicks and other fishy areas. He'll pick the fly pattern, describe the fishing technique, and tell you where to cast. After a successful day on the river you will have learned how the guide thinks and this experience will make you a better angler on the Madison.

Dead-drifted nymphs and dry flies can be especially effective when fished from a boat. The boat moves along with your fly, so it's easy to drift it into the boulders, eddies, slicks, and seams without drag. Unlike when you wade fish, cast your flies quartering downstream in order to get the longest possible drift. Strike indicators can be a big help. Some say it's cheating to use them, but some of us need all the help we can get. Once, Dave Whitlock was talking about strike indicators and one angler in the audience was becoming agitated and finally stood up from the back of the audience and said, "Well, how is that different from a bobber?"

Dave, never missing a beat, replied," "Well, for one thing, it goes through the guides a lot easier."

That was long before the advent of the big, fluffy yarn indicators that are so popular and effective these days. Maybe they are just a different breed of bobber, but it's an effective and fun way to fish nymphs.

Fishing dry flies from a moving boat affects fly selection. There are three fly characteristics that become key—visibility, floatability, and durability. Pick flies you can see, that float on the surface, and that last through many trout. Attractors work well on float trips. Good choices include Royal Trudes, Wulffs, H & L Variants, Stimulators, Goofus Bugs, and Double Wings. Low-riding patterns, with their low wings, are difficult to see. We tie special flies with high white wings for our float trips. It makes it much easier to see your fly.

When float-fishing during terrestrial time, fish patterns such as the Chaos Hopper, Foam Beetle, Lamar Cricket, and Zelon Flying Ant. These patterns all have a tuft of Hi-Viz or Zelon on top for better visibility.

No other insect creates as much frenzied excitement among anglers as the Salmon Fly. The Lyon to McAtee stretch has the most predictable Salmon Fly emergence on the river. For a few days in late June or the first week in July you can expect to have great fishing during "the hatch." Sometimes, bad weather and heavy runoff combine to scuttle the hatch. And some years caddisfly emergences bring up more fish than do the huge stones. But year in and out, on this section of river, the Salmon Fly hatch lives up to its reputation.

Important imitations include the Sunken Stone in gold and orange, size 6. The Little Yellow Stonefly, size 14, and the size-14 Stimulator work. Important nymphs include the size-4 Nature Stone and Brooks' Stone for the Salmon Fly and the Golden Stone. For fishing the Little Yellows have a bead-head Little Yellow Stonefly Nymph, sizes 12 to 14.

Over the last twenty years I've had great fishing when caddisflies and mayflies were on the water. In a good year the early Grannom or Mother's Day hatch, can be incredibly heavy from mid-May until the Spotted Sedge activity starts in late June. The Spotted Sedge starts just before the Salmon Fly hatch, and goes until early August. And the two species of Green Sedge important to anglers are prolific in July and September. The following patterns are affective: LaFontaine's Deep and Emergent Sparkle Pupa, in olive and gold, sizes 14 to 16; Iris Caddis, in amber, tan, and green, sizes 14 to 16; tan and olive X Caddis, sizes 14 to 18; LaFontaine's Diving Caddis, sizes 14 to 16, in olive and gold; and R.A.M. Caddis Larva, size 14.

Among the mayflies, the Western March Browns are on the water when the season opens and are active until the end of the first week in June. And Pale Morning Duns, Blue-Winged Olives, Flavs, and Slate Cream Duns (Pink Ladies) can emerge for several weeks.

Terrestrial patterns work well on this section. From mid-July until late October fish big grasshopper and cricket patterns in front of every boulder you can. When fishing the area around Ruby Creek, a few miles upstream of McAtee Bridge, try a size-4 Dave's Hopper in late summer. There are several boulders here that are cover to many large trout. The largest brown trout we have ever taken on the river came from this area a few years ago. Twenty-six inches long, it took a size-4 Dave's Hopper at the upper end of Ruby Creek Campground.

In the spring and fall streamers are productive. Olive and natural gray Woolhead Streamers and olive Woolly Buggers are good patterns, especially for brown trout—the rainbows prefer nymphs over streamers here.

Even in the turbid waters of the early season, I've had great success pitching size-2 streamers into the banks from a drift boat. Once the fly lands, let it sink for a couple seconds, then give it two short strips, pick it up, and cast it again. About once or twice a season is all I want to fish like this, but it is probably responsible for taking more big trout than any other method on this section of the Madison.

McAtee Bridge to Varney Bridge

This section of river—nearly twelve river miles—is open to angling all year. It lacks the huge boulders, slicks, and pocket water that characterize the Slide-to-McAtee stretch, but it has some huge trout. From McAtee Bridge to Indian Creek, wading is difficult. I broke one of my favorite rods here, slipping on the boulders and falling on the rod, shooting graphite splinters into my thumb.

The left side of the river, for a half mile below McAtee, is prime nymphing water. It also gets a good Mother's Day hatch, and in late June can be great Salmon Fly water.

A couple miles downstream is the site of one the most unusual catches I've seen on the Madison. Over twenty years ago Greg Lilly, Dave Corcoran, and I were on this stretch in early spring. Dave had just received a jolting strike as what appeared to be a huge brown trout swirled and took his big stonefly nymph. The big brown raced downstream, then came back up and nearly ran under the boat. The water was still discolored with snowmelt. As it approached the boat, it came to the top—a forty-pound beaver with the hook merely stuck in its furry coat. The hook came out, no harm to the beaver, much to our relief.

This section gets a heavy and reliable emergence of Salmon Flies and Golden Stones. Caddisflies and a couple of mayflies are also important at times. You can expect some Western March Browns and Blue-Winged Olives to come off in April and May. PMDs and Flavs appear in early July. And a few Slate Cream Duns emerge sporadically from July through the first week of August. Have size-20 to -22 Blue-Winged Olive nymphs, emergers, and duns, size-16 PMD emergers, nymphs, and duns, and size-14 to -16 Flav emergers and duns. Flav patterns will work for Western March Browns, too. Use the Sparkle Dun pattern to match the adult. Carry some rusty and olive Hackle Fiber Spinners in sizes 14 to 18 for the evening spinner fall.

Grannom caddisflies appear in mid- to late May. Spotted Sedges will be on the water at the end of June and will produce great evening hatches until August. And don't forget the two Green Sedge species. The first will come off the entire month of July, and the second appears from September through October. Have flies such as LaFontaine's Emergent Sparkle Pupa, sizes 14 to 16, in olive and tan, the size-15 to -17 amber, tan, and green Iris Caddis Emerger, and the size-14 to -16 tan and olive X Caddis.

But, for the most part, this section of the river is best for stonefly, attractor, and terrestrial dry-fly fishing, and if nothing is coming to the surface, big nymphs and streamers.

I love to fish a size-12 H & L Variant along the current seams and in front of rocks and boulders on this water. If that's not working, I'll pitch a size-4 Woolhead Streamer into the bank, lifting and maneuvering the floating fly line and fly so that it weaves in and out of boulders along the shoreline.

Float-fishing is the best way to fish this water—most of the section runs through private property. There is a great deal of unproductive water between good holding spots, so it's best to move downriver quickly and stop and fish the good water more thoroughly.

Midges can be effective, especially in midwinter. Midge fishing is best just downstream of McAtee Bridge on the left side of the river. Just before the diversion takeout, about two hundred yards below the bridge, you might see fish feeding on midges between noon and 4 p.m. Winter midge fishing is always chancy. Howling winds can make it tough to even open the doors of your car, let alone fish. But if the winds are down, try casting Griffith's Gnats to rising trout.

In midsummer you'll see a bright olive green scum on the river bottom, extending from the middle of the river toward shore. Trout will concentrate on the edge of this scum line. Every few hundred yards you'll find a notch of bottom free of scum. This spot looks like a V carved into the gravel along the green carpet on the river's bottom. Fish the V spot, and you can almost be guaranteed a nice trout.

About halfway to Varney, you'll come to an open, flat piece of water that appears to lack any holding water for good trout. This is Cameron Flats. At the Blue Moon Saloon in Cameron is a mounted rainbow trout of over ten pounds that came from this nondescript piece of water years ago. This stretch has a dozen or more places that will surprise you. Hire a guide, or spend many days on this water, finding such areas.

Near the end of this section, the river and surrounding landscape begin to change. Big cottonwoods line the shoreline, and deeper runs and holding areas start to hint at the water downstream.

VARNEY BRIDGE TO ENNIS LAKE

The fish in this section, mostly brown trout, are the biggest on the river. Float it and get out and fish the best water. This reach flows through private land, and access is limited to Varney, Eightmile Ford, Burnt Tree Hole, Ennis, and Valley Garden.

The water from Varney to Ennis Bridge is open all year. From Ennis Bridge downstream to Ennis Lake opens with the Montana General Fishing Season, the third week in May through February.

This water is nearly impossible to learn on your own. Even if you have your own boat, I recommend hiring a guide

The water in the Madison between Varney Bridge and Ennis Lake is more varied than that upstream between Varney and Quake Lake. In this photo you can see where the river begins to braid below Eightmile Ford access.

(Photo by Stan Bradshaw)

for the first few times on this section to point out what channels are best to fish and float, and which channel has a dangerous little dam.

The Varney section is much more varied than anywhere else below Quake Lake. The river braids around several islands, forming deep side channels. There are logjams, and the streamside vegetation is dense, with overhanging willows.

Even though brown trout predominate here, you are still likely to catch more rainbows than browns. You have to hunt the big browns to catch them. They hold much closer to cover—the deeper channels, undercuts, and holes. They are in the shade, alongside logjams, or under overhanging vegetation. Rainbows are in the middle of riffles and where currents and braids join below islands.

You also have a chance at Montana grayling in the Varney stretch. This rare fish inhabits some of the side channels just upstream of the Burnt Tree access and many of the channels from the Valley Garden access downstream to Ennis Lake, including the lake itself. If you see one rise you can nearly always take it on any fly even remotely resembling the natural insect. Grayling are rare, beautiful, and easy to fool. Handle them gently, and release them quickly. Their population fluctuates greatly on the Madison River.

The six miles from Ennis downstream to Ennis Lake has large islands, deep pools and undercuts, and many large trout. About half way down you come to Valley Garden, the only access point in this stretch. From below Valley Garden the river slows down and some of the side channels resemble large spring creeks. I've found that on many of the best looking pools I can't raise a trout; they seem fishless. Locals tell me that these pools hold huge browns that only come out at night. I believe them; on a few occasions I have hooked small trout and had them attacked by much larger trout.

Hatches in this section are scattered, sporadic, and limited. In the early season, the odd Blue-Winged Olive or midge emergence can bring up a few fish. Occasionally I have had great fishing during Western March Brown hatches in the early season. This hatch is unpredictable, but it doesn't take many naturals to trigger feeding. I've seen as few as twenty naturals on the water in an afternoon, and had good fishing by putting a size-14 olive Sparkle Dun in all the likely places.

Grannoms are on this stretch in May. If the runoff is heavy, the emergence and egg-laying might be strong, but the trout can't fight heavy currents to feed on top. When runoff is light, or late in coming, the Grannom can bring up great rises of trout. Then use a size-14 olive X Caddis on the surface or a size-14 dark olive Deep Sparkle Pupa for the subsurface. At times, the hatch can be so heavy that a pattern like the Royal Trude occasionally works much better than a closer imitation. The attractor gets the attention of the trout.

Salmon Flies, Golden Stones, and Little Yellow Stoneflies show up in late June. Your best approach is to float this stretch in order to find surface-feeding fish. Have patterns such as Brooks' and Nature Stone Nymphs, sizes 4 to 6, and Little Yellow Stonefly Nymphs in regular and beadheads, size 12. On the surface, flies such as Sunken Stones work best in size 6. A size-14 Yellow Stimulator works fine for the Little Yellow Stones.

In July look for the Great Gray Spotted Sedge along the shore. The trout love this huge—size-10 to -12—caddisfly, but seldom take the adults from the surface. This caddisfly has a bright olive body with a dark mottled wing. Use a size-10 olive brown Free-Living Caddis Larva, a size-10 brown/bright green Deep or Emergent Sparkle Pupa, and a size-10 brown/bright green LaFontaine Diving Caddis.

There are two important net-making caddisfly species in this section during summer evenings. The larger Spotted Sedge emerges in good numbers, but as the summer progresses, a closely related genus, the Little Sister Sedge becomes even more important. This insect is a size 16, with ginger wings and a tan body. This contrasts to the size-12 or -14 body and brownish wings of the Spotted Sedge. During heavy hatches or egg-laying flights, when both caddisflies are abundant, the trout can become selective to one or the other.

Spotted Sedge and Little Sister Sedge are numerous from July to mid-August on this section. Every warm, calm evening look for these size-14 brownish-yellow caddis and size-16 tan caddis to emerge and bring up the trout. Use a pale green, brown/yellow, or tan Iris Caddis and LaFontaine's Emergent Sparkle Pupae, sizes 14 to 16. Use a size-16 tan X Caddis to imitate the adults. Egg-laying

Spotted Sedge and Little Sister Sedge females are easy to see because they fly low over the water and bounce along on the surface. A great pattern to imitate this activity is an Elk Hair Caddis in sizes 14 to 16.

PMDs, Blue-Winged Olives, and Small Western Green Drakes are plentiful on this stretch. Sparkle Dun and Cripple PMD, Flav, and Blue-Winged Olive (*Baetis*) patterns, as well as emerger patterns, match these insects. For PMDs use size 16, Flavs sizes 14 to 16, and Blue-Winged Olives sizes 20 to 22. Sizes-14 to -16 Hackle Fiber Spinners, in green and rusty variations for the PMDs and Flavs, are a must for July and August evening fishing. Many times you'll come upon fish quietly sipping spinners off the surface between 7 and 9 in the evening. Often these spinner falls are those of fast-water species such as Slate Cream Dun and Western March Brown. Be prepared.

This section is great terrestrial water. Grasshoppers, leaf hoppers, beetles (some of them huge), crickets, bees, flying ants, and other insects may bring up fish all season long. The best time to fish these insects is in the heat of the summer—late July through early September. A good float-fishing rig is a beetle and hopper combination. From 9 to 11 a.m., the trout gently sip beetles, ignoring the hopper. Then, around 11 a.m. to noon, the winds crank up and the fish start looking for hoppers. This activity lasts until 4 or 5 p.m.

While few people fish streamers on this stretch, they are productive. The big browns in this reach are always looking for sculpins, juvenile whitefish, and small trout, and might take size-4 Woolhead Streamers and Fly Fur Streamers that imitate these young fish.

ENNIS LAKE

Ennis Lake was formed by a dam in 1906. It's shallow, the deepest part not twenty feet deep. Many felt that the lake would be dead by this time. Charlie Brooks in his book *The Living River*, said that Ennis Lake would heat up to over 90 degrees by 1980, killing any and all trout in it.

Some twenty years after the predicted doom, this lake is still productive. I recently fished it with Dick McGuire, and we had a good time with some of the lake's rainbows. Trout were rising to *Callibaetis* and Trico emergences.

During the summer of 2000, one of the warmest ever on record, water temperatures in Ennis Lake remained cool enough for surface-feeding trout. Montana fisheries people tell us that when water temperatures rise near seventy degrees trout quit feeding and become stressed. This did not happen on Ennis Lake, nor on the river above the lake. New flow regimes recently instituted out of Hebgen Lake may be the answer, keeping water temperatures lower during the heat of the summer.

Whatever the reason, Ennis Lake is still fishing well. Its not as good as Hebgen or Quake Lakes, but for those living near it, it's just fine. You can wade fish nearly the entire lake. McGuire calls it his big wading pond. I've been with him, wading and fishing, over a mile out into the lake.

You'll need *Callibaetis* Sparkle Duns, Shrouds, Foam Hackled Spinners, and a *Callibaetis* Nymph, all in size 16. Tricos should have olive bodies to imitate the female dun, in sizes 18 to 20. An olive-bodied Trico Sparkle Dun works just fine. I'd also have a size-10 olive Beadhead Damselfly Nymph.

ENNIS LAKE TO THREE FORKS, MONTANA

For years, few anglers fished this stretch. Many felt the river warmed up too much during the summer months. Most of us fished this reach during the winter on the way home from a trip to Bozeman to visit the dentist, renew our driver's license, or go to an evening movie at a real movie house.

The first ten miles of nasty white water immediately below Ennis Dam is for expert floaters only, but you will find good fishing, floating or wading, downstream from the rapids all the way to Three Forks.

(Photo by Stan Bradshaw)

For the first ten miles below the dam, the river runs through the Bear Trap Canyon–Lee Metcalf Wilderness area. It is canyon water at its best. Do not even think of floating this nasty stretch unless you've been through it with a licensed outfitter a time or two, and are an accomplished white-water boater. One of the rapids, called the Kitchen Sink, is a more than a handful even for white-water experts, and has killed a number of floaters.

You can fish the canyon from Bear Trap Canyon Road, which runs alongside the river for several miles between Norris and the Black's Ford Access. Or take the North Ennis Lake Road south off Bear Trap Canyon Road at the Bear Trap Bridge, halfway between Norris and Black's Ford Access on the river. This road follows the east side of the river upstream into the canyon.

Early-season streamer action can be great. Use sculpin imitations, such as the Woolhead Streamer, in brown or olive, sizes 2 to 4. Many years ago a local minister and I went to Black's Ford Access in April. It was a bright day, and along the way Frank insisted we let him net a few sculpins for bait. I bet him that I could outfish him with my flies. He took the challenge, although I could see him, as a man-of-the-cloth, wince at the idea of a bet. I won, he bought lunch, and I converted him to fly fishing.

In the fall, streamers, grasshoppers, and beetles are all effective. You'll do best on this reach if you can float it, but when insects such as caddisflies, mayflies (specifically the Blue-Winged Olives), and midges are active, I prefer to wade it. Cover very little water, concentrating your time and effort to those areas that are convenient and slow enough to allow the fish to comfortably rise to the insects.

During the summer months, from mid-July through August, fish the upper river, above Ennis. If you're in the area in the early or late season, give this section a try. At first, it may seem nondescript and puzzling, mostly long riffles and glides. A good guide can help you solve it.

You can find good fishing all the way to Three Forks. Trout populations are low compared to the upper sections of the river, but fishing can be great, especially when the upper stretches are covered in snow.

Early season dry-fly action gets going in January, when midges are active in the afternoon hours, and lasts to late May. Blue-Winged Olives appear in early April and continue through May. And the Mother's Day hatch, the Grannom, comes on strong a few weeks before Mother's Day every year. And to complicate the fishing, the banks of the canyon are lined with trees infested with small green caterpillars—size-16 insects that drop onto the water constantly in early May.

The Mother's Day hatch, common everywhere in the Rocky Mountains, dominates the fishing simply because of the incredible blizzard of insects. The Madison emergence can be reliably fished every year because, unlike the Yellowstone, runoff usually comes after the hatch. The emergence lasts from the end of April through mid-May, and once the insects start coming the trout readily feed on them.

Both the emergence and egg-laying phases of the Grannom carpet the water with naturals. Often, several-inch-thick mats of naturals will raft up along the shoreline and back eddies. Fishing is best in the afternoons, when trout feed on both emerging pupae and spent adults. Imitations such as the size-14 brown/bright green Deep Sparkle Pupa and Emergent Sparkle Pupa, and the size-14 dark Elk Hair Caddis and the brown/bright green EZ2C Caddis are effective. Sometimes it's best to present a fly that doesn't even imitate a natural. To compete with the hordes of naturals for the trout's attention, use down-wing patterns, such as Royal Trudes, Double Wings, and Stimulators, that are visible and still mimic the caddis silhouette.

After the fishing season closes in Yellowstone Park, you can still find great dry-fly fishing from November through February when the midges are active. This angler is braving the cold near Raynolds Bridge.

CHAPTER 2

Seasons of the River

 INTER

When most fly fishermen think of fishing the Madison River around West Yellowstone, they think of the summer months. The weather is consistently good, insect emergences and dry-fly fishing is great, and there are lots of anglers on the river. But there is plenty of great fishing at other times of the year, when the river receives far less fishing pressure. By mid-September the kids are back in school, evening frosts and even a snow storm or two appear, and the casual anglers have headed home. The fall run-up fish, spawners from Hebgen Lake, come into the river in big numbers, and Blue-Winged Olive emergences bring trout to the surface.

The season closes for the year in Yellowstone Park on the final Sunday in November, but from Hebgen Lake downstream there can be some great dry-fly fishing when midges are active from November to February. The midge hatches are the most consistent hatches of the year, as far as getting head-and-tail risers to the surface. You can have the river to yourself at this time, although the weather may be a little unpredictable. Midge patterns should include size-18 to -22 Griffith's Gnat Emergers and standard Griffith's Gnats in sizes 16 to 20.

Streamers also produce well during the winter. I like to present a size-6 olive or brown Woolhead or Fly Fur pattern in all likely holding spots along the shoreline, behind boulders, in the seams and merging currents, and in front of log-jams. Because the water temperature is colder in the winter, work your streamer slowly, without any induced movement. The best method is to cast upstream on a short, tight line.

Nymphing is also effective in winter. I like a two-fly setup with a size-4 to -6 stonefly nymph on top and a small midge pupa or mayfly nymph trailing behind. Stonefly nymphs are active in winter when the water is warmest during the day. Around two o'clock in the afternoon, these large nymphs crawl out from under their rocky hiding spots to graze on algae. Trout look for stonefly nymphs from about 2 to 4 p.m. in winter. The trailing midge pattern should be a size-16 to -20 Krystal or standard Serendipity. This pattern works best to imitate midge larvae and pupae that are taken by trout in winter months.

SPRING

On sections of the Madison that are open to fishing in winter and spring, midges will continue to bring trout to the surface when spring arrives the end of March. Have size-20 to -22 Griffith's Gnat Emergers, and size-16 to -20 Griffith's Gnats and Zelon Midge Clusters.

In April the early *Baetis* emergences begin. This hatch continues for several weeks, into late May. Have size-20 to -22 *Baetis* Sparkle Duns and Knocked Down *Baetis* Duns and size-18 to -20 Pheasant Tail or *Baetis* Nymphs.

In late April the first caddisflies appear in the Bear Trap Canyon of the Madison, all the way downstream to the town of Three Forks. The famous Mother's Day caddis hatch, the common Grannom comes off a few weeks before the Mother's Day holiday rolls around. It works its way upstream and if weather and stream conditions remain stable, without much cold spring runoff, the caddis may come off upstream to McAtee Bridge.

If its been a warm spring with no cold runoff, look for the March Brown mayflies to emerge along the river in late April and early May. Size-14 olive Sparkle Duns are a good match.

The same nymphs and streamers that are effective in winter will work in spring too. Add a size-12 Little Yellow Stone beadhead and Beadhead Prince Nymphs to those winter selections.

In June runoff usually hits its peak. But it's unpredictable. If you're thinking of fishing the Madison during June, call before making the trip just to ensure sure current water conditions make it worth the effort.

The effects of runoff show up strongest below the West Fork of the Madison. When snowmelt comes into the West Fork it pours tons of silt and mud into the river. The main stream is turbid all the way downstream to Ennis Lake. When this happens, work the river upstream of the West Fork with nymphs and streamers. Generally by the first week of July runoff subsides, the water clears, and dry-fly fishing begins.

UMMER

During the last week of June the big stonefly hatches appear. The Salmon Fly and Golden Stoneflies bring anglers from around the world to fish the river.

A river's entire stonefly population doesn't hatch at the same time. Stoneflies begin to emerge in the lower reaches of the river and the hatch works its way upriver, slowly moving a few miles a day. The hatch first appears in Bear Trap Canyon below Ennis Lake, and then moves three, four, or more miles upstream daily, until two weeks later they reach Hebgen Lake. Because the river runs much warmer in the Park, the Salmon Fly hatch comes off earlier, around the first week of June.

Good flies to have for the Golden Stonefly and Salmon Fly hatches are Brooks' Stones, Natural Drift Stonefly Nymphs, Kaufmann Stones, and Nature Stonefly Nymphs of both species, sizes 4 to 6. For adults, you'll want Golden and Salmon Fly Sunken Stones, sizes 4 to 6, and size-4 to -8 Stimulators in yellow and orange, and size-6 Flex-Stones.

Beginning in early July and extending through the rest of the summer season several species of little yellow stoneflies appear. These insects run anywhere from size 12 through size 18. On bright sunny days, when no other insects are on the water and these stones can be seen drifting in good numbers in the riffles and pockets, you can take trout on an imitation. Use a size-12 Little Yellow Stonefly Nymph in beadhead or standard style, a light Hare's Ear Nymph in size 12, or dry flies including size-12 to -16 Stimulators, Yellow Air Heads, or Little Yellow Stoneflies.

All during the Salmon Fly and other stonefly hatches, caddisflies will be emerging heavily too. The Madison River is a caddisfly river. On pleasant summer evenings from July until September, caddisflies fill the air, and wild-rising brown and rainbow trout feed in every pocket, pool, and seam along the Madison. In summer, the evening caddisfly activity gets going around 9 p.m. and might last as late as midnight. Never leave before 9:30. Important summer caddisfly patterns include the Deep Sparkle Pupa and Antron Caddis Pupa, sizes 14 to 16, in olive, brown, and gold; Iris Caddis Emergers, sizes 15 to 17, in pale green, tan, and amber; X Caddis, sizes 14 to 18, in olive and tan; tan Elk Hair Caddis, sizes 14 to 16; brown/yellow EZ2C Caddis, sizes 12 to 14; and light ginger Diving Caddis, size 16.

Mayflies are important during the summer too. Big Green Drakes, medium-sized Pale Morning Duns, fast-water March Brown duns, Slate Cream duns, and Blue-Winged Olives all bring trout to the surface. These emergences and their evening spinner falls are complicated by the Madison's microhabitat, microdistribution features. Many times, particularly during evening hours, you'll come upon what looks like a huge caddisfly emergence. Thousands of caddis flying about and trout rising everywhere. You put on a caddis and get refusals. When this happens look to the sky; you'll likely see hundreds of mayfly spinners hovering above the river. Then check the trout's rise forms and you'll note that most are quiet sips, or you'll see just the snouts of larger trout as they tip up slightly to take in mayfly spinners.

Then there are midges and terrestrials that bring up the summer's trout. In early summer it seems time is always on your side; the season is young and many more hatches and rising trout are yet to come. Before you know it, it's late summer and the hatches are starting to wane. This is when terrestrials—grasshoppers, bees, beetles, ants, and crickets— become important. If you plan to fish from Quake Lake downstream to Ennis during mid- to late August, make sure you have flying ant patterns. You'll need them.

Few consider the summer as a time to pitch streamers, but the Madison is packed with sculpins and juvenile whitefish. On those days when all the classic dry-fly tactics fail to move fish, prospecting with streamers can save your day.

 ALL

Fall is a glorious time to fish the Madison River. Gone are the lines at gas pumps, grocery stores, and the two stoplights on main street. Locals can reclaim "their" seats at the restaurants and "their" parking spots along favorite stretches of "their" trout streams. Bugling bull elk have gathered their harems in the early morning fall light. The hoarfrost is heavy on golden grass along the river where serious anglers work the riffles and pools. And thick clouds of mist float up and down the river's silver course.

By mid-September the upper river in Yellowstone Park fills with run-up brown and rainbow trout. And the lower river fishes well on top with terrestrials, the late Green Sedge, and fall Blue-Winged Olives that begin emerging in September.

To the surprise of many visiting anglers, late fall can be the best time to fish terrestrials on the Madison. Most think that the first few frosts of the late summer and early fall kill off the grasshoppers. These little guys are tough. I've seen hoppers in November at 9,000 feet. The afternoon sun heats up south slopes and the snow melts off around tree trunks or along rocky faces. Next thing, I see and hear hoppers clicking and flying around attempting to find a mate—all after several inches of snow and freezing nighttime temperatures. Hopper fishing can go through October, and the same with bees, beetles, ants, and crickets.

The Barns Pools yielded this fall spawner.

(Photo by André and Linda Altans)

In mid-September, the "Morning Midge" activity begins on the Madison below Quake Lake. On most mornings, from 9 a.m. to noon, you can fish this black and white midge that most anglers incorrectly identify as a Trico. At casual glance it does resemble a Trico in flight, its trailing antennae taking on the appearance of the Trico's long tails. A black Zelon Midge, size 20, is the only pattern you'll need to imitate this insect.

Late season *Baetis* emergences can be impressive. One November, I hit the Madison at $3.00 (Cliff-Wade Lake) Bridge. It was dead calm, in the mid-thirties, and I was there by noon, in plenty of time to fish the emergence. I stopped on the bridge to look at the water from the warmth of my truck. Rising fish were everywhere in the pockets just above the bridge. By the time I rigged and got on the water a north wind started to blow, and so did the snows as the temperature dropped like a rock.

I decided to stay close to the truck so I could keep the engine running and the heater on "Hot." I fooled several nice trout, enough so that my hands got wet and I got cold and had to go back and forth to my vehicle to get warm between trout. It's amazing what one goes through to catch and release a few fish.

There are several good areas to fish late season *Baetis* on the Madison. The upper river in the Park is always good. The river below Quake Lake offers spotty fishing; the current speed and depth is often too great to allow trout to feed on the tiny insects. Trout will instinctively not use more energy in chasing tiny flies than they get from eating them. Prime spots for late season action are at Raynolds Pass and $3.00 Bridge, just above and below McAtee Bridge, and just below Varney Bridge. Much of the slower water stretches just below Bear Trap Canyon downstream of Ennis Lake are also prime *Baetis* habitat.

Fall fishing with big streamers, soft hackles, and stonefly nymphs is legendary all along the Madison. Hearty anglers fish in all kinds of weather from sleet and snow to warm and dry during this favorite time. Good patterns include size-4 to -6 Woolhead and Fly Fur Streamers, size-14 Pheasant Tail Nymphs, size-12 to -14 Partridge and primrose Soft Hackle flies, and size-4 to -6 Nature Stone Nymphs and Brooks' Stones.

So you can see, there is fishing all year long on the Madison River. And some of the best times are when few anglers are on the river—spring, fall, and winter.

Landing a Salmon Fly–caught rainbow

CHAPTER 3

Salmon Fly Hatch

*T*he most famous insect emergence in the West is the Salmon Fly (*Pteronarcys californica*). It's huge, and it triggers a real feeding frenzy when it's good. No other insect creates as much excitement with fly fishers year after year. During the annual Salmon Fly hatch, anglers from across the globe assemble to follow and fish "The Hatch." Fishing access sites along the Madison look like flea market parking lots. Campgrounds and motels are jam-packed. And fly-fishing guide services have been booked solid for months.

In most years many anglers are disappointed. Rainy or snowy weather, heavy runoff, and sporadic concentration and emergences of insects combine to produce frustrating angling. But when the hatch is good, it's unbelievable. Hitting it right once in several seasons makes it all worth the effort, money, and time.

To hit the hatch right, you need the right conditions. If you want to fish dry flies the water has to be running fairly

During the Salmon Fly hatch, anglers from around the globe follow and fish "The Hatch" from one end of the Madison to the other. Conditions aren't conducive to a good hatch every year, but when they are, its unbelievable.

(Photo by Glenda Bradshaw)

clear. Occasionally trout will come to the surface for the huge insects even when the water is cold and turbid. But prime dry-fly action comes with clearer water. The air and water temperatures can get too warm also. If they do, the emergence can blow up and move too quickly upstream. In low-water years, I've seen the hatch shoot upstream ten miles or more in one day. Ideally, you want it moving up three to five miles daily. You do not want miserably cold days either, because then the hatch will dribble off. You hope for cool nights, clear, warm days. It is much better to have windy conditions to knock the adults into the water and get the fish looking for them. To get all those things together with a good emergence is really tough.

There are several strategies that can be used to fish the Salmon Fly activity. Often I'll fish nymphs ahead of the hatch. Trout are always on the lookout for nymphs migrating to the river's shore prior to emerging. This is the most reliable fishing during this time and sometimes the only fishing to be had if the water is too turbid. Nymphs like Brooks' Stone, Natural Drift Stonefly Nymph, Nature Stone and Kaufmann Stone in sizes 4 to 8 work great.

The best dry-fly fishing takes place when the females return to the water to lay their eggs, several days after emerging. Swarms of females fly upstream over the river, fluttering and bouncing on the surface to release their eggs. They are clumsy fliers and afternoon winds along the Madison often knock the adults to the water prematurely and keep them skittering, skating, waking, and thrashing on the surface. So don't be afraid to impart a little action to your fly occasionally.

As with the emergence, egg-laying flights move upstream a few miles every day. Finding the exact place where the females are gathered is critical to successful dry-fly fishing. If you're too far upstream of the flights, the trout won't be keyed into the adults yet. Too far downstream and the fish are likely to have gorged on the naturals and be uninterested in feeding. Floating the river increases your odds of finding the egg-laying females and surface-feeding trout because you can cover a lot of water.

If you get to the middle of the hatch, you might catch a trout that is regurgitating Salmon Flies. When you find this, pack up and try another spot because you won't have good fishing here; it's hard to take burping trout.

Sometimes I like to fish the Madison as many as ten days behind the hatch. The fish are looking for the big bugs again and you can have most of the river to yourself as most anglers are chasing the top end of the emergence. This method is especially effective once the hatch gets to McAtee Bridge. When the emerging bugs pass McAtee, the head of the hatch usually blows upstream ten or more miles a day. No one seems to know why. It can be tough to figure just where the head of the hatch is, or where the egg-laying might take place. But if you fish several miles and days behind the hatch, you don't get caught in that guessing game, and you're likely to find some of the best fishing of the hatch.

I like to approach from straight downstream when wade fishing during Salmon Fly activity. I use a short-line upstream cast to the bank or holding water. Trout are often suspicious of adult flies. Huge naturals floating along on the surface sometimes appear to unnerve the fish. You'll get many refusals, and trout will follow your pattern downstream, slapping and bumping your fly with its nose. If I come upon a trout that refuses my fly, I rest him for a minute and then cast at his holding area again and twitch my fly as it gets near his spot. This will sometimes provoke a vicious strike.

Its a good idea to carry a few types of adult Salmon Fly patterns. Use a high-floating fluttering type when insects are skittering on the surface on windy days and the trout are chasing them. A size-4 Stimulator or Henry's Fork Stone are good for skittering, waking, and moving on the water. The Flex-Stone, a jointed pattern that bends with every twist of the current, is good for fooling selective fish.

When the naturals are skittering and egg-laying and the trout are chasing them everywhere, fish the entire river, even the heaviest flows. It's exciting to fish the middle of the river, where the rough and tumble currents crash into boulders. I'll heave a size-4 Stimulator out into these flows and sometimes a huge trout, one that usually takes only sculpins or whitefish, comes out and nails the big dry. The big stonefly can bring big trout to the surface.

If I'm fishing behind the emergence and egg-laying flights, I prefer a low-riding fly like a greased size-4 to -6 Sunken Stone or Henry's Fork Salmon Fly. These flies float with a low silhouette and are gently taken off the surface by trout. Since the egg-laying occurred days before, trout are very suspicious of high-floating, skittering patterns. Now they look for flies awash in the surface film, or even beneath the surface. Year in and out more large trout will take a Sunken Stonefly than all other patterns combined. Trout take these large insects underwater after the hatch has passed.

If there is one rule of thumb for fishing the Salmon Fly hatch, it is this: Be flexible and don't get caught sticking with just one method. What worked yesterday won't today, count on it. There's never telling what tactic may take fish on any given day.

Look for smaller stoneflies to bring up trout during Salmon Fly time too. Golden Stoneflies (*Hesperoperla pacifica*) may not be as numerous as Salmon Flies, but they can bring on great fishing. The Goldens are a size smaller, size 6 to 8, than the big Salmon Flies, but at times, they can bring up more trout. They emerge a week or two later than the Salmon Flies. Use the same strategies as for the Salmon Fly, with the same fly patterns tied smaller.

And Little Yellow Stoneflies, *Isoperla* sp. and *Suwallia pallidula*, will bring trout to the top, too. These smaller stones, sizes 12 to 16, emerge from early July into August. It is not unusual for trout to key on the smaller stoneflies, refusing larger Golden or Salmon Fly imitations. Have size-12 to -16 Yellow Stimulators, yellow Air Heads, and Little Yellow Stoneflies for these times. An effective nymph pattern includes a size-12 to -14 light Hare's Ear Nymph.

Keep in mind that even though this is stonefly time, about half the time some other insect is going to dominate the fishing. Usually that insect is one of the caddisflies. Never underestimate the importance of caddisflies on the Madison River. And, with caddisflies in the mix, you can pursue a specific strategy: Early in the morning, when adult Salmon Flies haven't begun to move, use nymphs. When the hatch begins switch to dries. On a typical day the trout will stay on dry flies until 4 to 6 p.m. Then suddenly someone throws the switch and the Salmon Fly activity shuts off. By 7 p.m. the caddisflies come on and the trout then go to Spotted Sedge emergers and crippled adults. This might last until 10 or 11 p.m.

Pay attention to rise forms. Fish feeding on Salmon Flies usually don't come completely out of the water. If fish are feeding on caddisflies, you'll see small trout leaping out of the water. Pay attention.

FISH SALMON FLIES AT NIGHT

There's one thing to remember during Salmon Fly time on the Madison: Between Lyon Bridge and Slide Inn, the big adults often emerge at night, especially if there's a bright moon. Since the adults emerge at the shoreline, put on a Salmon Fly dry around 10 p.m. and fish it on this stretch when the hatch is here. The river is too dangerous to wade after dark, so splat your flies along the banks and streamside boulders. Use short leaders and tippets to 2X and, in most years you'll have great late-night fishing.

The Madison is a great caddisfly river and the Raynolds Pass area (above), is a good place to fish them on warm, cloudy afternoons.

(Photo by Rowan Nyman)

CHAPTER 4

Caddisflies

*A*s we discussed above, never underestimate the importance of caddisflies on the Madison River. Even during good Salmon Fly emergences and egg-laying flights trout may prefer Spotted Sedges, Green Sedges, and Great Gray Spotted Sedges over stoneflies.

The Madison is a classic caddisfly river. It's full of riffles. It has tremendous water quality, is well aerated, and experiences little harmful winter ice scouring. As a result, the river is prime habitat for several caddisfly species. We have net builders, free-living, purse-case, saddle-case, and tube-case families. As a result, caddisflies are the most important insect to the fish, and fishermen, on the Madison. And yet they are the insects least understood by most anglers.

Gary LaFontaine, in his great book *Caddisflies*, gives three clues to these hatches on rivers: Trout can be seen leaping out of the water; there are no insects on the water; and most of the rises in the faster currents are bulging and splashy. In the slower currents look for quieter dimples, porpoising rolls, and tails that barely break the surface. It is important to consider rise forms when deciding what the fish are taking, but never wise to make a judgment based solely on them.

A key caddis opportunity occurs when the females return to the water to lay their eggs. Females might bounce, skitter, and flutter along on the surface, dive beneath it, or float flush in the surface film. You might even find spent females on the surface. Learn when and where to expect caddisflies and how to recognize caddis behavior.

The early season emerging Grannom (*Brachycentrus occidentalis*) is often referred to as the Mother's Day caddis because it hatches during late April and early May. It is most important on the lower river, below Ennis Dam and downstream to Three Forks. On years with little early runoff or when the spring thaw is late, I've seen great emergences above Ennis Lake, all the way upstream to the West Fork of the Madison. On the river in Yellowstone Park, this insect comes off from opening day in May to July 4.

The Grannom is large, size 14 to 16, and appears almost black. It is dark gray in color, with a distinct olive stripe on the side of its body. The Grannom is most active in the afternoon and evenings. Good flies for *Brachycentrus* are size-14 to -16 olive Deep Sparkle Pupae and Emergent Sparkle Pupae, Antron Caddis Pupae, and olive X Caddis in sizes 14 to 16.

The big, sprinting Great Gray Spotted Sedge (*Arctopsyche grandis*) at size 8 to 12 is the largest caddisfly to emerge in quantity on the Madison River. They emerge from late June to late July. The adults run about madly on streamside boulders, going nowhere, yet covering a lot of ground.

This species is mostly nocturnal, and only adult and larval patterns are important to anglers. Both are good searching patterns for heavy, rough water. Trout love the big, juicy bright green larvae. And because the larvae move so much, fish take imitations readily.

From Raynolds Pass to Varney Bridge it is common to see many adults running on the banks on warm, cloudy afternoons. Because of the large number of naturals and their size you'd expect to see heavy hatches and egg-laying flights along with lots of rising trout. I've never seen either an emergence or an egg-laying flight. And, I've not seen trout feeding on either stage exclusively. It's my guess that emergence and egg-laying are done at night. It is important still to recognize adults, and to know when they are running the river banks. Good fly patterns for this caddis are the size-10 bright green Caddis Larva and size-10 to -12 bright olive X Caddis.

Of all the caddisflies, the Spotted Sedge (*Hydropsyche* sp.) is the most important to fly fishers on the Madison. It may be the most important insect of any type—including mayflies, stoneflies, and midges—on the river. From Quake Lake to Ennis, no other insect comes close to the Spotted Sedge for providing continuous fly fishing.

From late June to the end of August in the evening you'll see thousands of these insects over the surface of the river. The adults are sizes 14 to 16 and have brown wings early in the season and tan wings later in the season (many caddisflies go from dark to light as the season progresses) and light greenish tan or golden yellow bodies.

My favorite strategy in fishing the evening caddis is to arrive on the river around 7 p.m. and look for pockets or slicks behind large boulders. You'll see a few small trout rising in the faster currents, splashing and bulging after emerging pupae. Its always tempting to cast to these risers, but you might spook the larger browns and rainbows that will come up later. Be patient. At dark, around 9 p.m., even the quiet water along the shoreline comes alive with subtle dimples and tails that barely break the surface as big trout rise to emerging Spotted Sedge. The emergence can last well past dark, and the trout continue to feed on these insects as long as there are naturals available. They'll hatch as late as 11 p.m. on the Madison in July and early August.

The best patterns to imitate Spotted Sedge are LaFontaine's Emergent Sparkle Pupa and the Antron Caddis Pupa both in a brownish-yellow body, size 14. An Iris Caddis Emerger in pale green, amber, or tan is deadly, sizes 15 to 17. The best dry fly for imitating crippled caddisfly adults is the X Caddis, sizes 14 to 16 with a gold or tan body. And a size-14 to -16 tan Elk Hair Caddis does a fine job imitating egg-laying caddisflies on the surface, but sometimes the fish really focus on the underwater egg-layers and a size-14 to -16 brown/yellow Diving Caddis works well.

The Little Short-Horn Sedge (*Glossosoma montana*) emerges sporadically, yet can be important below Quake Lake in July. This size-20 caddisfly with a gray body and wings can be tough to predict because its emergence varies yearly. Still, have a few pupae imitations of this little guy. Occasionally its emergence overshadows that of the Spotted Sedge. Good imitations include size-20 black LaFontaine Emergent Sparkle Pupae and Antron Caddis Pupae, and size-20 black X Caddis.

The Long-Horn Sedge (*Oecetis disjuncta*) is important in the Park and below Quake Lake. It's a full size 16, with a golden yellow to bright green body and a tannish-gray wing. You can't miss the antennae on this caddisfly, which is two to three times its body length. You'll see it in the Park in late June. Below Slide Inn I've fished egg-layers from mid-July to the first of August. Use the size-16 LaFontaine brown/bright green Emergent Sparkle Pupa and the Spent Sparkle Caddis.

The long-emerging Little Plain Brown Sedge (*Lepidostoma pluviale*) appears for as much as an entire month, from mid-

July to mid-August. These size-18 caddisflies have olive bodies and brown wings; the males always sport a dark gray
recurve on the leading edge of their wings. This caddisfly
usually comes off in the evening, but I've fished good emergences on warm cloudy afternoons around the West Fork.
Trout relish emerging pupae and adults. The emerging adults
ride the current for several seconds after hatching. The larger
fish prefer pupal imitations, and emergences can be heavy
with rises of big trout.

The egg-laying phase of the Little Plain Brown Sedge
will also bring up big fish. During this phase, the adults
ride the surface passively during afternoon and evening. The
emergence and egg-laying phase may occur simultaneously.
This is a good time to seine the surface and the top two to
three inches of water with a small aquarium seine to find
out which phase predominates. The pupa has undeveloped
wings while the adult's are fully developed. An imitation of
an adult is likely to take more trout, but larger fish are
selective to the pupa, so it pays to be aware of individual
preference. Good patterns are a size-18 LaFontaine
Emergent Sparkle Pupa, an Antron Caddis Pupa, and a size-
18 olive X Caddis.

Two species of Green Sedge, *Rhyacophila bifila* and *R.
coloradensis*, are important on the Madison. I refer to them
as the Cro-Magnon Caddis. In caddisfly evolution, advance-
ment is measured in part by the insect's ability to build a
protective case for its larvae. The Green Sedges don't build
cases. The larvae freely roam about on the bottom. This
makes bright caddis green larvae important to anglers. It's
one of the most useful searching patterns known.

The adults are available to trout from early summer to
fall. Adults of both species range from size 14 to 16, same
with the larvae. Adults have an olive body and distinctly
mottled gray and black wings.

My friend, Dr. Charlie Cummings and I were fishing grasshoppers on the Madison near the Grizzly Bar one early September day a few years ago. After lunch we took a break, discussing bonefishing and bird dogs, when a few trout began to rise. They were taking egg-laying Green Sedges that were dancing about in the heavy flows. At first only smaller trout came to the surface, slashing after the ovipositing females. But soon larger trout began to rise, taking the naturals as they drifted calmly in the quiet flow near shore. We took turns fishing our X Caddis to the larger trout on the bank. When you fish the Green Sedge, look to the river's edge for the big bank feeders.

The early species, *R. bifila* appears on the Madison below Quake Lake anytime in July and August. The later species, *R. coloradensis*, comes on in September in the Park and below Hebgen Lake. Some good patterns include the size-14 to -16 Caddis Green Larvae, size-14 to -16 LaFontaine brown/bright green Emergent Sparkle Pupa, and size-14 to -16 olive and bright green X Caddis. For the underwater egg-layers use the size-14 to -16 gray/bright green LaFontaine Diving Caddis.

The June Pale Morning Dun hatch brought this brown to the surface to take a PMD imitation.

CHAPTER 5

Mayflies

There are a few things you should know about mayfly emergences on the Madison. One of the most important is that the heaviest mayfly hatches usually take place on overcast, rainy, or snowy days. Mayflies suffer more emergence injuries and tend to ride the water longer before taking off during nasty weather. As a result, the fish have a better chance to feed on them. And, trout are less spooky under overcast conditions.

BLUE-WINGED OLIVE

The first important mayflies of the season to emerge are the Blue-Winged Olives. Two species of this mayfly are important. The first to emerge is *Baetis tricaudatus* and it comes off below Ennis Lake in early April. Above Ennis Lake it usually emerges around May 1. The second species is *Baetis punctiventris*, which hatches in the Park around June 1. Both species peak in May and June, then again in September and October. Both species are sizes 18 to 22.

Baetis tricaudatus hatches bring many trout to the surface, and larger trout frequently feed on nymphs and crippled duns. While coloration varies widely, grayish olive is most common. This mayfly emerges best on overcast days from noon to 4 p.m. If it's bright and sunny the hatch will be sporadic.

From Raynolds Pass Bridge to the West Fork is my favorite place to fish this hatch. But there are several other good places to fish it. You'll find good hatches below Ennis Lake and the Bear Trap Canyon, and in the channels stretch below Ennis, just upstream of Ennis Lake. In Yellowstone Park the best emergences occur between Seven Mile Bridge and Riverside Drive and on meadow water below Madison Junction.

The overriding consideration in fishing *Baetis* emergences is current speed. While emergences might be heavy along the entire river, trout will only feed on them where they can do it economically. Fish never use more energy feeding on insects than they gain. So the fish feed in smooth, moderate flows.

B. tricaudatus hatches can be so heavy that your fly might have a tough time competing with the naturals. And, trout can get so confident and locked onto nymphs that one might take your nymph, hook itself, and continue to feed as long as you don't put pressure on it.

For both insect species I like to use nymphs and knocked-down dun patterns, and Sparkle Duns. From Raynolds Pass Bridge to the West Fork of the Madison, Blue-Winged Olive spinners are required. I like a size-20 green Sparkle Spinner. A Diving Blue-Winged Olive Egg-Layer matches the underwater activity and it's effective near the end of the hatch.

The smaller species, *B. punctiventris*, emerges only in the Park. Look for it in June and again in September and October. Use size-18 to -22 Pheasant Tail, Pheasant Tail Twist, and *Baetis* Nymphs; size-20 to -22 *Baetis* Sparkle Duns and Emergers; size-20 *Baetis* Cripples, Knocked Down Duns, Sparkle Spinners; and size-18 to -22 Diving Blue-Winged Olive Egg-Layers.

With the Blue-Winged Olive, you can often fish the entire emergence with a nymph because the larger trout commonly stay keyed on them. You'll see big trout aggressively slicing after nymphs, their backs breaking the surface, and you might think they're on the duns but they will mostly be nymphing. If you see the dorsal fin and tail, but no nose, keep fishing a nymph.

There is one special situation with the *Baetis* that gets little attention from most anglers. The egg-laying females go underwater to paste their eggs on the bottom. Strangely enough, when they go subsurface, the males also go underwater with them. This creates a "super" spinner situation—it isn't like the spinner fall of any other mayfly species, where only the females are available to the trout. The fish take advantage of this abundance of food by gorging on the underwater *Baetis* adults.

The Diving Blue-Winged Olive Egg-Layer, with a wing of clear Antron, looks just like the bright adult mayfly underwater. It's designed to be fished dead-drift like an upstream nymph, often as a dropper pattern behind a dry fly. At the end of the regular *Baetis* hatch, when the egg-laying often starts, the Diving Blue-Winged Olive Egg-Layer can be really effective.

WESTERN MARCH BROWN

There are three species of March Brown (*Rhithrogena* sp.) on the Madison. Some people also call them the Early Light Olive Dun.

The first species is the *R. morrisoni*. When runoff doesn't wash out the emergence, this insect can bring on good rises of trout. If the river is turbid, this large mayfly won't be a factor. If the water is clear the trout usually rise to this hatch even though it is seldom heavy. *R. morrisoni* only hatches from Hebgen Dam downstream. It appears in May. A size-14 to -16 olive Sparkle Dun works best.

Two other species, *R. futilis* and *R. undulata* emerge in such sporadic numbers that their dun stages are seldom important. But their spinner falls can be heavy and can trigger great rises of trout on the warm, calm evenings below Quake Lake from mid-July to late August. Use a size-16 rusty Sparkle or Foam Hackled Fiber Spinner.

PALE MORNING DUN (PMD)

Two species of Pale Morning Duns, *Ephemerella infrequens* and *E. inermis* are important on the river. Since both species look and act alike we can treat them the same. From opening day in late May to mid-July the PMDs will bring up lots of fish in the Park. From the outlet of Quake Lake to Ennis Lake, PMDs will appear from late June to mid-August.

The nymphs are usually a dark amber to chocolate brown, sizes 16 to 18. Duns range from lime green in the Park, to pale yellow elsewhere, in sizes 14 to 18. The duns' wings are usually the same color as their bodies. PMD spinners are rusty or olive, with clear wings, sizes 16 to 18.

Trout take the nymphs as they ascend to the surface and drift in the film just before hatching. Larger trout from Slide Inn to Ennis prefer drifting nymphs over swimming nymphs.

Crippled duns are common during a heavy emergence. Trout seem to recognize this vulnerability and key in on these injured duns. And spinner fall can be important in the morning and evenings.

PMD activity is predictable and consistent. You can count on them if weather conditions are right, and they emerge at the most comfortable time of the day. In the Park in June they'll come off around 11 a.m. On the lower river, below Quake Lake, they emerge around 9 a.m. to 10 a.m. on warm days in July.

During "perfect" fishing weather (rain, sleet, or snow) in the Park, I've fished PMDs from 11 a.m. to 6 p.m. as wave after wave of insects came off the water. So don't take the term *morning* too seriously.

Spinners usually fall best on warm, calm mornings from 9 a.m. to noon, and evenings from 7 p.m. to 10 p.m. Trout can be difficult to take during the spinner falls. They prefer an olive spinner, but will sometimes take size-16 rusty spinners.

Most often large rainbows and browns will be selective to one stage of the PMDs. If you notice duns drifting over fish and the trout taking them, you obviously can assume they are on duns. If you see noses, heads, and backs breaking the surface, you know the fish are on duns. If they let duns pass by, then try nymphs. If you see fish tails, the fish are taking nymphs.

The best flies to use for Pale Morning Duns are size-14 to -18 PMD and Pheasant Tail Nymphs, size-16 to -18 PMD Emergers and Cripples, size-16 to -18 PMD Sparkle Duns and Knocked Down Duns, and Sparkle and Foam Hackle Fiber Spinners, sizes 16 to 18.

SMALL WESTERN GREEN DRAKE

Small Western Green Drakes (*Drunella flavilinea*), called Flavs, are important on the Madison River below Quake Lake. It emerges from about July 10 until early August. Flavs are big, robust insects, size 14 to 16. They have olive bodies and dark gray wings. The water near ($3.00) Cliff-Wade Lake Bridge is best for this hatch.

The timing of the hatch varies considerably, depending on the weather. On warm, sunny days look for it around 8 p.m. On rainy and cool days it'll be on the water around 5 p.m., sometimes earlier. The hatch often brings up nocturnal browns more than it does rainbows.

The nymph phase of the Flav doesn't seem to be important on the Madison. An olive Sparkle Dun, size 14 to 16, is my favorite fly for this hatch. And, even though Flavs do not seem to be as prone to emerging injuries as other mayflies, large trout always seem to like crippled emerger flies best. So include some Flav Cripples, Knocked Down Duns, and Pistachio Cones in sizes 14 to 16.

Flav spinners fall in evenings and can bring on good rises of trout. Carry a size-14 to -16 olive Sparkle Spinner and you'll be prepared. But the spinners are usually outgunned by caddisfly emergences, so don't leave your caddis patterns at home.

GREEN DRAKE

The huge Green Drake (*Drunella grandis*), occurs between Hebgen and Quake Lakes, and between Slide Inn and the West Fork. On a good year you might only see a hundred or so of these mayflies, but they make big trout stupid. It never takes many duns of this size to bring up good trout.

Look for them in early July between the lakes. On the lower river you might meet them in mid- to late July. Carry Green Drake Sparkle Duns, Emergers, and Cripples in size 12. A size-10 slate/olive Mess and a size-12 Pistachio Cone matches the dun and emerging nymph of this mayfly, and they are effective when they are fished together in a two-fly rig.

PINK LADY

The Pink Ladies (*Epeorus albertae*), are common but sporadic emergers below Quake Lake. Don't ever expect to see the water covered with these size-14 olive mayflies, but don't ignore them either. Pink Ladies are big enough to bring fish up, and I've had great fishing when they are on the water during July and August. I prefer a size-14 olive Sparkle Dun for fishing this hatch. You'll find the Pink Ladies on the water around 6 p.m.

TRICORYTHODES (TRICOS)

Tricos (*Tricorythodes minutus*) are important only on Hebgen and Ennis Lakes, and upstream of Hebgen into the Park. Most of the fish rising to the Tricos are whitefish but you'll find some trout among the feeding whitefish. Cast your flies only to trout, rather than shotgunning your casts into pods of whitefish and hoping for a trout.

Tricos on Hebgen and the Madison are larger than on most other waters. They will run as large as size 18. The females, with olive bodies, are the most important to imitate. Focus on the Madison Arm of Hebgen Lake and on the river from 6 a.m. to 9 a.m. Look for places where the currents or winds concentrate mayflies. Trout will sometimes rise to clumps of spinners; a size-14 Griffith's Gnat tied with black palmered hackle will imitate these clumps.

The Tricos emerge on the lakes from late June to August. On the river they emerge from mid-July to mid-September. Use size-18 olive Sparkle Duns, size-18 to -20 Gulper Specials, and size-20 black Trico Sparkle Spinners.

SPECKLED-WING SPINNER

The Speckled-Wing Spinner (*Callibaetis ferrugineus hageni*), is important on Hebgen, Quake, and Ennis Lakes. It has a brown body and speckled wing and is a size 16. Trout feed on the nymphs, duns, and spinners.

Callibaetis brings trout to the top when it hatches in May, and during its next brood from July to September. The emergence begins around 10 a.m. and may continue until 2 p.m., if conditions allow. Look for spinners to fall at the same time.

If the wind churns the lake into a chop, go to the leeward side to find at least a thin band of flat water. The trout won't rise to *Callibaetis* duns or spinners in rough water, but they will feed on drowned insects. A classic wet fly, such as a Blue Quill, can catch fish in a wind. Good patterns for fishing Speckled-Wing Spinners are size-16 *Callibaetis* Nymphs, Shrouds, Sparkle Duns and Cripples, and Foam Hackled Fiber Spinners

See Chapter 1 to find a more specific discussion of *Callibaetis* tactics on Hebgen Lake.

CHAPTER 6

Midges

Wherever trout are on the Madison, or in the lakes, so are midges. Too often we underestimate their importance on rough and tumble rivers like the Madison. Most anglers avoid fishing midges. But trout like them, so come to the Madison prepared to fish them.

Midge activity on the river is localized and extreme microdistribution is the rule. You can walk the banks for miles without seeing one adult. Then you come upon slicks behind boulders and quiet pockets loaded with midge mating clusters and trout rising to them. Look for water no more than a foot deep with slow stretches. Trout will be in thin water, searching for midge pupae and adults in the surface film.

Midging trout are tough to approach. Often you'll get one cast over the riser and you'll put him down. Midge dry-fly fishing is major league stuff on the Madison; it's on-your-knees with short, pinpoint casts, drag-free floats, long leaders, and fine tippets.

Midges in Hebgen Lake are as huge as size 12. Smaller midges along the river are as small as the size-22 Morning Midge of the fall.

Midges are most important during emergence when trout rise to pupae and crippled adults. Between Slide Inn and Three Forks, trout key on clusters of mating midges.

On Hebgen Lake focus on midges for a month after the ice comes off, from early May into June. While they can be important year-round on the lower river, the best time to fish them is in September and October, and in the winter.

The best flies for midging activity are the size-12 to -16 Krystal Serendipities in red and pearl, size-18 to -22 Variegated Midge Larvae, size-18 to -22 Zelon Midges and Griffith's Gnat Emergers, size-18 to -22 Improved Buzz Balls, and size-16 to -20 Zelon Midge Clumps and Griffith's Gnats.

CHAPTER 7

Terrestrials

When most anglers think of terrestrial time on the Madison River, they think of grasshoppers. There are plenty of other terrestrials that bring trout to the surface. While they are largely overlooked, these other terrestrials might be more important that grasshoppers.

Terrestrials have no "emergences" or corresponding rises of fish. And rarely will anglers come upon activity of any terrestrial insects heavy enough to cause a concentrated rise of trout. There are a few exceptions: migrations of Mormon Crickets, flying ants and mating bee swarms, and grasshoppers that have migrated to lush streamside vegetation after the benchland above the river has dried out can create fabulous feeding sprees.

On the Madison you must always be ready to fish terrestrial flies. I've taken trout on black beetle imitations every month of the season because they're recognized as food to trout, and can be found near and on the water at any time.

The same with ants. I once saw a brown trout about twelve inches long rising, actually climbing along and onto a log that was in the river near the West Fork. The trout would rise slowly, high up onto the log, then slide down its length, dropping back fully into the water. Then it would scoot below the log, and sip, sip, sip something off the surface film. At first I thought this fish was sick. But it kept repeating this routine. I presented several flies to this trout—grasshoppers, caddisflies, mayflies, spinners, and other flies. I couldn't fool it. Finally, I had all I could take. I waded in and put it down. The log was crawling with huge black ants. This fish was knocking the ants off the log to feed on them.

Grasshopper activity is strongest during the heat of summer, but I've taken trout from May to November on hopper flies. Hoppers are present in good numbers for much of the season. They're like miniature armored cars. They can hunker down and endure snow and cold, reappearing when the weather warms up again. Only a blanket of snow and several days of cold will kill them.

Hopper fishing kicks in during a warm, strong wind—a "hopper wind." Without the wind, stay with anything but grasshopper flies.

The best hopper patterns ride low in the surface film. Patterns like Dave's, Chaos, and Parachute Hoppers are best in smaller sizes—12 to 14. For a big pattern, something that might bring up the largest trout in the river, try a Flex-Hopper.

One of the most important terrestrials on the Madison is usually among the most overlooked. The tiny leaf hopper is always present along the edges. From mid-July through September a size-18 to -20 lime green X Caddis imitates it well, along with doing double duty as a microcaddis imitator.

Swarming bees and flying ants can bring huge rises of trout in mid- to late August. Look for flying ants and swarming bees from Raynolds Pass Bridge to Ennis Lake. Carry

This trout still "wears" the cricket fly that caught it.

some size-12 Killer Bees and size-12 to -16 cinnamon and black Foam Flying Ants.

Crickets, both regular and the huge Mormon types, are all along the river. In August you'll hear, and sometimes see, these insects. Female Mormon Crickets reach a full three inches long and big fish feed on them. I enjoy pitching huge imitations like the Lamar Cricket, sizes 4 to 6, into the heaviest flows of the river in late summer.

We also get a good crop of caterpillars on the river. In the summer you'll see small green caterpillars, and a size-12 green Woolly Worm or Deer Hair Wooly imitates them. In the summer, late August and September, the classic woolly bear worms are seen. They're big and black in color with a brown middle band, and they are fuzzy. They bail out of streamside willows and other vegetation into the river. They're a big bite of protein, so trout feed on them. You can fish them floating or sunken. You'll do well with a size-6 Woolly Worm, unweighted, that imitates this creature.

But for me, beetles, both large and small, produce more quality trout every summer than all other terrestrials combined. I've taken trout, big trout, on beetle imitations every month of the fishing season. It's very important to fish beetles at the edges and where overhanging vegetation drapes over the water, where trout expect to see them. The pockets, seams, foam lanes should all be searched with size-10 to -18 black Foam Beetles. A good trick for broken water is to fish a sunken terrestrial, such as a beetle like size-12 to -16 Black June hair wing wet fly, dead-drifted along the bottom.

Tie your imitations with enough bulk and underbody that the fly lands on the water with a distinct "plop." Beetles come onto the water with a splat or plop. I like to use a peacock herl underbody, or I'll tie a thick foam underbody.

When fishing terrestrials, I fish the edges and overhanging vegetation, where trout expect to see naturals. One exception is in the late season. So much bank walking occurs during terrestrial time that trout might head to the security of deeper, rougher water in the late season. Try placing your terrestrials in the heaviest, deepest flows of the river. The areas that seldom fish well before late summer seem to come alive. Try longer casts, and throw a loop of slack into your cast to allow the fly to drift as long as possible. Fish the white water and heaviest flows, prospecting around boulders, logjams, and small islands.

Sunken terrestrials such as ant, beetle, hopper, and bee patterns are more often effective than high-floating flies. Try a two-fly setup with a floating grasshopper or cricket trailed by a sunken ant or bee. Let the hopper fly be your indicator.

Be flexible during terrestrial times. Try different flies, different holding water, times of day, and other sections of the river. If drag-free drifts don't produce on your hopper or cricket, try twitching your fly.

CHAPTER 8

Attractors

hile matching specific hatches is clearly key to successfully fishing the Madison, attractor patterns should still be an important part of your arsenal. Royal Wulffs and Trudes, Double Wings, Turck's Tarantulas, Goofus Bugs, H & L Variants, Stimulators, and other attractor patterns remain some of the biggest selling flies in the West Yellowstone area, primarily for the Madison River. Royal Wulffs and Trudes, sizes 14 to 16, are still the best-sellers in August, no doubt because they imitate so well the red flying ants important on the river then.

Attractors are especially effective when float fishing, when you get one attempt at a given spot. Attractors seem to pull fish more quickly to the surface than do most imitative patterns. As a result, they are well suited to the one-shot opportunities you get float fishing.

Always match the color of your attractor to the kind of day you're fishing. On a bright, sunny day, use a Royal Trude or Wulff, or a Royal Double Wing. On a gray day, use a gray Wulff, gray Trude, or a Lady Heather. In the evening, try an orange Stimulator or an orange Double Wing, matching the warm light of the sunset. Match the color of the fly to the intensity of the sunlight.

CHAPTER 9

Dry Fly Methods

While streamers and nymphs are every bit as deadly (and some would say more deadly) as dry flies, many of us spend most of our efforts fishing on the surface for the aesthetics and fun of it. Following are a few basic guidelines to improve your success rate on dry flies.

Wade as little as possible. It amazes me to see anglers literally running into the heavy water of the Madison with arms flailing to keep their balance. This does little but spook many trout, and risks a dunking.

Never string your rod at the parking spot; pick a place where you can sit and look over holding water as you assemble your equipment. This way you can watch the water for insects and feeding trout, and check wind conditions. Check along the river for any caddisflies, mayflies, stoneflies, midges, or terrestrials such as ants, beetles, or hoppers.

Keep your casts short, under thirty feet. For most of my fishing I'll cover the Madison with upstream casts of fifteen to twenty feet. This enables me to pick up and recast after the fly has traveled just beyond the rising fish, allowing me to present my fly again without spooking it. I also can get back to the fish without false casting or wasting time stripping in slack. The longer you cast, the less control you have of your line. And on the Madison, with its rough and tumble, riffle character, the trout are easily approached. By scooting along on your knees or backside, you can get to within a rod's length of holding trout. You can even dap for trout in the Madison if you are careful and get into position. Make it a game, to see how close you can get to rising trout and still have them rise to your fly. That's part of the fun.

If nothing's hatching, pick a dry fly that imitates an insect the trout recognize. On the Madison that might be a black beetle or Spotted Sedge (*Hydropsyche* sp.) rather than a cicada or *Hexagenia* pattern that they've never seen before and won't recognize as food. Pick something that's been on the water recently.

Sneak along on the banks, keeping low and out of sight. Wade only when you can't cover a hold or explore a seam from shore. Fish every holding area and pocket slowly, being careful not to disturb the water.

With increased fishing pressure I spend more of my time trying to fool individual rising trout, rather than prospecting for a willing trout in the next pocket. An exception might be an expected hatch, particularly mayflies. Because of extreme microdistribution of some of the Madison's hatches, you'll want to explore more water when you expect a hatch.

When fishing mayfly hatches, figure out which stage of emergence the trout are feeding on. Then position yourself about fifteen feet downstream of the rising trout. Pinpoint your casts. The trout work in narrow feeding lanes and will not move for a fly. And since the wind always blows on the

Madison River during mayfly hatches, get as close to the fish as possible to minimize the wind's effects on your cast.

The broken water covers the rolling, turning motion of fish taking emerging nymphs in the surface film. Many trout, especially larger ones, will let duns pass and feed exclusively on insects trapped half in and half out of the water. If you see this type of feeding, switch to an emerger, knocked-down dun, or floating nymph and drift it in the surface film at the same level that the trout are working.

Count the times between a trout's rises to see if there is a rhythm. This will allow you to anticipate his next rise, and time your cast accordingly.

When fishing from a drift boat the best position will be from the side closest to shore. Short casts, from fifteen to twenty feet, are always the best. Keep your fly in close to the bank unless you are fishing to a riser away from the shoreline.

The best way to fish trout feeding on caddisflies is to make short, upstream presentations. This eliminates casting across the river's mixed currents, and reduces drag. And you can get much closer to rising trout by approaching them from downstream.

Fishing caddis pupa imitations dry works best for large trout when they feed on these pupae. Some argue that an across-and-downstream presentation works best, but I feel that this method causes too many break offs, and larger trout like their pupa imitations fished dead-drift.

If you have a tough time keeping track of your pupa imitation in the film, tie on a high-floating adult caddis pattern, such as an X Caddis or Elk Hair Caddis. To the bend of the dry fly attach a 12-inch tippet, and then tie on a low-floating pupal pattern. The higher floating adult caddis imitation is your indicator.

When the wind is blowing a gale downstream, and the insects are fighting to fly upstream against it, face downstream. Put on a buoyant fly, such as an H & L Variant, and cast down and across, holding the rod high, letting the fly kick at the end of the line so that it's bouncing all the way across the currents. Don't even cast; simply hold a blow line and let the fly kick in the current. Pick pockets, pulling in a little bit of line, and letting a little out. With this technique you can pick a line of river below you and thoroughly cover it.

CHAPTER 10

Nymph Tactics

The Madison River is a great place to learn nymph fishing. On the slow section in the Park the trout's take can be hard to detect. Below Hebgen and Quake Lakes the water moves so quickly that when a fish takes your fly the line tip really jumps upstream.

Nymphing is the most productive method you can use to catch fish on the river. The key to effective nymphing on the Madison is to get close to the fish. Keep your casts as short as possible, preferably ten to fifteen feet—never beyond thirty feet because line control becomes a problem, and the fly comes off the bottom.

I don't like strike indicators, especially those huge fluorescent plastic bobbers referred to as "strike indicators." They're unsightly litter when discarded at streamside. And they mesmerize anglers into inattentiveness or loss of concentration. Many anglers so depend upon the bobber's overt movement to indicate a fish's strike that they fail to see the more subtle take of larger trout. Anglers with failing eye-sight have an excuse. This is the only time I recommend using the bright orange, lime, or yellow fluffy indicators made of poly yarn.

An alternative to the yarn indicator is a big dry fly as a strike indicator. Simply tie on a section of tippet to the dry fly at the bend with a clinch knot, then knot the nymph to the end of this tippet. The tippet length depends on the depth and speed of the river. I never go longer than three feet. Use a big hopper or cricket, and often the trout will take your indicator fly.

When caddisflies, mayflies, midges, or tiny terrestrials are on the water, use a crippled adult as an indicator and tie on a trailing pattern such as an emerger, pupa, or nymph. And, when caddisflies and mayflies are both on the water, try imi-tations of each. This often allows you to determine which stage or insect the trout are feeding on at any given moment.

The most effective nymphing method is the short-line technique in which you concentrate on the tip of your line to locate the drifting nymph. With a little practice you'll be amazed at how this allows you to clearly see things under-water. Soon you'll be watching trout inspecting or even tak-ing your nymph in the currents, seams, and pockets. And you will pick out holding trout in even the heaviest currents, adding another dimension to your enjoyment.

When fishing mayfly nymphs or caddisfly larvae or pupae on the Madison's pocket water, use a different tactic than you would use on a smooth meadow-water stretch. On the rough pocket water, approach from directly below working trout. Try to get within fifteen feet of the trout to eliminate as many currents as possible between you and the fish and to improve casting accuracy. During heavy mayfly emergences trout lock into narrow feeding lanes as they feed on nymphs and emerg-ing duns. Getting close to the fish makes it easier to pinpoint

Fish nymphs on a short line, concentrating on the tip of the line to locate the drifting nymph. When the line stops, you may have a fish. Or it could be snagged on the bottom. Try again!

your casts. Short cast are also easier to manage in the wind. If you're using caddis larval patterns, weight them, because the larvae don't swim.

Always use a floating line when nymphing. Sinking lines will tangle around everything in the stream. If you need to get the fly down in the current, add weight to the leader.

Fishing big stonefly nymphs is one of the most productive ways to fish the Madison. As with caddisflies and mayflies, always fish upstream, dead-drift. Use a short, heavy leader and tippet. Weight your flies and leaders so the fly bounces downstream, hitting the bottom where the fish see the naturals. I like to walk my nymph back to me by giving it a 10- to 15-foot upstream cast and throwing in a loop of slack at the same time. The slack allows the fly to sink to the bottom. If the fly hangs up on the bottom, I lift the line and leader from the water and raise the fly just enough to bounce and walk it back to me. Charlie Brooks popularized the "Brooks' method," one similar to what many anglers today call "high-stick nymphing." This is an effective technique for fishing huge stonefly nymph patterns. The term *high-stick* comes from the line control phase of fishing out your cast when nymphing with heavy nymphs in heavy currents. First cast your fly upstream ten to fifteen feet. As fly and line move downstream towards you, keep the rod tip pointed above the spot where the line enters the water. This keeps drag to a minimum, you're in touch with your nymph at all times, and you can set the hook quickly when trout takes. Lift the rod tip so that only a slight sag is in the line between the rod tip and the water. On short casts, the lift of the rod tip need only be about waist high to take up the slack. On longer casts you must stretch you arms high overhead to do the same thing. I love to use this method in early spring with a size-4 to -6 Brooks' or Nature Stonefly nymph with a Deep Sparkle Pupa trailing behind. Sometimes the trout take my heavily weighted stonefly pattern, but usually, even though there may not be any caddisflies on the water, fish will take the Deep Sparkle Pupa.

I use soft hackle flies a lot on the river, usually fishing them like traditional nymphs. A drag-free float is always most effective for larger trout, and I seldom use any weight when fishing soft hackles. Sometimes I like to present an upstream cast up to thirty feet long. Then, keeping my rod tip high and stripping in slack I keep in touch with my fly and direct it into slicks, around boulders, through pockets and holding lies as it works its way back downstream to me. I can steer it and work it into all likely holding areas by keeping tight line control.

CHAPTER 11

Fishing Streamers

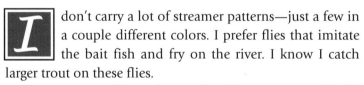I don't carry a lot of streamer patterns—just a few in a couple different colors. I prefer flies that imitate the bait fish and fry on the river. I know I catch larger trout on these flies.

One pattern I like is the Woolhead streamer, specifically the Woolhead Sculpin. The other important streamer is the Fly Fur Streamer. We tie this fly to imitate rainbow and brown trout juveniles, as well as bait fish such as the Utah Chub.

The Woolhead is best fished in the spring and fall, before and after most insect activity on the river. One year I fished this pattern all season just to see what I could do with it. I found the size of the sculpin imitation wasn't critical, but coloration was. In the Madison there are two important sculpin colors: olive brown and mottled dun.

It's best to fish sculpin patterns upstream, dead-drift, just like you would a big stonefly nymph. I always approach and cover the river initially from the downstream, short-line cast position. This approach makes the streamer appear vulnerable. The sculpin is a poor swimmer. When dislodged from the bottom, it puts its large pectoral fins up and turns slightly, causing it to fall back towards the bottom, like a fighter plane turning into a dive. Present a sculpin fly like the natural would act, and do it on a short, tight line so you can see and feel the take of the trout.

Most bait fish and juvenile trout are too agile to interest large trout. A predator will instinctively not expend more energy in capturing a meal than it gains from eating it. So, when fishing a Fly Fur Streamer imitating a young rainbow or brown trout or chub, cast upstream, retrieving the streamer back as if it was injured and barely hanging on to life. Make it hard for a large trout to pass up this hurt creature.

CONCLUSION

s I sift back through these last chapters, I realize I've said: "the Madison is a great dry-fly river," "the Madison is a great nymph river," "the Madison is a great streamer river." All these statements are true. The Madison fishes anyway you want it to. If you come and want to fish nothing but dry flies for twelve months of the year, you can do it. You *can* take fish on dries all year. There's really only a week or so out of an "average" year when the river is in runoff and dry-fly fishing would be unproductive. The same holds for nymphs and streamers.

And one cannot own a river or even a small part of it, except in one's heart. The Madison River is a big part of my heart. I know the river, and I love it. I hope you'll share it one day with me, soon.

APPENDIX 1

Hatch Chart

MAYFLIES

BLUE-WINGED OLIVE   *Baetis tricaudatus & B. punctiventris*
Hook = 16–22, Body = olive, Wing = dark gray

WESTERN BLACK QUILL   *Rhithrogena morrisoni, R. futilis, & R. und*
Hook = 12–14, Body = purplish black, Wing = dark gray

PALE MORNING DUN   *Ephemerella inermis & E. infrequens*
Hook = 14–18, Body = yellow olive, Wing = light gray

WESTERN GREEN DRAKE   *Drunella grandis*
Hook = 10–12, Body = dark olive, Wing = dark gray

SMALL WESTERN GREEN DRAKE   *Drunella flavilinea*
Hook = 14–16, Body = dark olive, Wing = dark gray

SPECKLED-WING SPINNER   *Callibaetis ferrugineus hageni*
Hook = 14–16, Body = gray, Wing = speckled

TRICO   *Tricorythodes minutus*
Hook = 18–22, Body = dark gray, Wing = light gray

CADDISFLIES

GRANNOM   *Brachycentrus occidentalis & B. americanus*
Hook = 14–16, Body = greenish brown, Wing = varies from brown to gray

SPOTTED SEDGE   *Hydropsyche cockerelli, H. oslari, & H. plac*
Hook = 14–16, Body = yellowish brown, Wing = mottled brown

GREAT GRAY SPOTTED SEDGE   *Arctopsyche grandis*
Hook = 8–10, Body = olive brown, Wing = dark gray

LITTLE SISTER SEDGE   *Cheumatopsyche campyla*
Hook = 14–16, Body = olive brown, Wing = brown

The Madison encompasses many different types of river habitat as well as three lakes. This hatch chart lists only the most important aquatic insects, the super hatches that a fly fisherman should be ready for because trout will turn selective. The dates blocked out on the calendar cover the heavy hatch periods for each insect. The brief descriptions of the adult stages of each will allow you to carry at least a generally matching pattern.

APRIL	MAY	JUNE	JULY	AUG	SEPT	OCT	NOV
••••	••••	•			••••	••••	•••
		••	••••	•••			
		•••	••••				
		••	••••				
			••••	••••			
			••••	••••			
			••	••••	••••		
	• ••••		••••	•			
	••	••••	•••				
		•••	•••				
		•••	••••	•••• •			

CADDISFLIES (CONT.)

GREEN SEDGE *Rhyacophila bifila & R. coloradensis*
Hook = 14–16, Body = bright green, Wing = mottled gray and brown

LONG-HORN SEDGE *Oecetis avara & O. disjuncta*
Hook = 14–16, Body = ginger, Wing = ginger

DINKY PURPLE-BREASTED SEDGE *Psychomyia flavida*
Hook = 18–20, Body = purplish brown, Wing = brown

LITTLE BLACK CADDIS *Glossosoma montana*
Hook = 20–22, Body = grayish black, Wing = grayish black

LITTLE OLIVE CADDIS *Lepidostoma pluviale*
Hook = 16–18, Body = olive, Wing = brown

STONEFLIES

SALMON FLY *Pteronarcys californica*
Hook = 4–8, Body = orange, Wing = dark gray

GOLDEN STONE *Hesperoperla pacifica*
Hook = 6–8, Body = light ginger, Wing = ginger

LITTLE OLIVE OR LITTLE YELLOW *Suwallia pallidula*
Hook = 14–16, Body = bright yellow, Wing = light gray

YELLOW SALLY *Isoperla* species
Hook = 14–16, Body = yellow, Wing = light yellow (straw colored)

TWO-WINGED FLIES

MIDGES Diptera species
Hook = 14–22, Body = black, olive, or brown, Wing = light gray

APRIL	MAY	JUNE	JULY	AUG	SEPT	OCT	NOV
		••	••••	••••	•••		
		••	••••	••••			
			•••	••••	••••	•	
		••	••••				
			••	••			
		••	••••				
			••••				
			••••	••••	••		
			•••	••••			
		ALL YEAR					

APPENDIX 2

Popular Flies for the Madison River and Hebgen, Quake, and Ennis Lakes

*T*reat this list as a framework rather than a must-have set of flies. Work from it to fill your boxes during the winter, or if you don't tie, purchase a workable selection. You will not need all of these patterns at any given time or on any given section of the river. You can match how, when, and where you intend to fish to put together your own pattern list. Shops in the area sell most of these flies and many are available through mail order.

Should you bring favorite patterns from your home waters? Absolutely. A good fly will work anywhere. The same imitations and attractors that fool trout in the East, West, or South will take the rainbows and browns of the Madison. At the same time, don't ignore the local killers—flies that have proven themselves on the river.

DRY FLIES

MAYFLY PATTERNS

SPARKLE DUNS:

Baetis 18–22	*Rhithrogena* 14–16	**Pale Morning Dun** 14–18
Green Drake 10–12	**Flav** 14–16	*Callibaetis* 16 **Tricos** 18–22

CRIPPLES AND EMERGERS: same sizes

SPINNERS: Hackled Spinners for *Rhithrogena*, *Callibaetis*, and Tricos in same sizes

SHROUD: 16 (for *Callibaetis*)

CADDISFLY PATTERNS

X & IMPROVED X CADDIS:
Brachycentrus 14–16 (olive) *Hydropsyche* 14–16 (tan) *Arctopsyche* 8–10 (olive)
Rhyacophia 14 (green) *Oecetis* 14 (green) *Glossosoma* 20–22 (black)
Lepidostoma 16–18 (olive)

EMERGING & SPENT CADDIS:
Iris Caddis for *Hydropsyche* 14–16 (or 15–17 if using TMC 102Y hooks)
Spent Sparkle Caddis for *Hydropsyche* 14–16 (tan)
Spent Caddis for *Oecetis* 16 (green or olive)
Spent Caddis for *Lepidostoma* 16 (olive)

OTHER GOOD CADDIS PATTERNS: Elk Hair Caddis 10–18 (olive and tan)
CDC Hair Caddis 14–18 Stimulators 12–16 (yellow)

DRY FLIES (CONT.)

STONEFLY IMITATIONS

Nick's Sunken Stone 6–8 (orange and golden)
Henry's Fork Stone 6–8
Little Yellow Stonefly 12–16
Flex-Stone
Stimulators 6–16 (yellow)
Works well when trout are taking all species of stoneflies skittering–egglaying.

MIDGE PATTERNS

Standard Griffith's Gnats and Emergers 16–22
Zelon Midge 20–22
Improved Buzz Ball 14

TERRESTRIAL IMITATIONS

Chaos, Dave's, and Parachute Hoppers 8–14
Black Crystal and Foam Beetles 10–16
Black, Red and Black, and Cinnamon Ants 12–18 (standard and flying ties)
Killer Bee 12–14
Cricket 12–14
Slough Creek Cricket 6–8
Foam Beetle 12–18
Deer Hair Wooly 12–16
Black June 12–16

ATTRACTORS AND GENERAL FLIES

Royal Wulff 8–18 (tied with high wings)
Royal Trude 10–16
Horner Deer Hair (Goofus Bug) 8–18
H & L Variant 10–18
Adams 10–20 (standard and parachute style)
Double Wing 8–10
Yellow Air Head 12–16
Lady Heather 10–14

HIGH FLOATING EXCITERS

Variant 10–12   Deer Hair Skater 10–12

STREAMERS

Woolhead Sculpin 2–6 (brown and olive)
Rainbow and Brown Trout Fly Fur Streamers 6–8

ATTRACTORS

Glow Bug 6–10 (pink, lime, orange)   San Juan Worm 8–12

GENERAL

Woolly and Flash-A-Buggers 2–8 (live, black, yellow–brown)

NYMPHS, PUPA-LARVA, AND EMERGERS

MAYFLY IMITATIONS

Baetis Emergers and Nymphs 18–22
PMD Emergers and Nymphs 16–18
Green Drake Emerger 12
Flav Emerger 16
Callibaetis Emergers and Nymphs 16
Pheasant Tail Nymph 12–20
Pheasant Tail Twist Nymph 14–20
Diving Blue-Winged Olive Egg-Layer 18–22
Slate/Olive Mess 10   Pistachio Cone 12

CADDISFLY IMITATIONS

R.A.M. Caddis Larva 12–16
Serendipity 14–16 (olive, brown, crystal, lime)
Deep Sparkle Pupa 12–16 (olive, tan, gray, bright green, amber)
Emergent Sparkle Pupa 12–16 (olive, tan, gray, bright green, amber)
Antron Caddis Pupa 14–18 (brown and olive)
Iris Caddis 13–17 (TMC 102Y) 14–16 (TMC 100 or 5210)
                    (amber, olive, and natural tan)
Free-Living Caddis Larva 10 (olive brown)
Diving Caddis 14–16 (ginger, brown/bright green, brown/yellow)

STONEFLY IMITATIONS

Nature, Brooks', and Kaufmann Stones 4–8 (golden amber and black)
10–16 (yellow or amber stone bead heads)
Natural Drift Stonefly Nymph 4–8 (black) 8–10 (golden)

OTHER INSECT IMITATIONS

Olive Crane Fly Larva 10–12
Serendipity 14–18 (olive, lime, red, and crystal) Serendipities represent caddis, midge,
and mayfly larvae, pupae, and/or nymphs extremely well.
Variegated Midge Larva 18–22

SOFT HACKLE PATTERNS

Partidge and Orange, Pheasant Tail, Fall, Partridge and Herl, Starling and
Herl, Nick's 10–16 (tan or green)
Works well fished during the fall prespawning times or anytime!

GENERAL

Hare's Ear Nymph 12–16   Pheasant Tail Nymph 12–20
Red Squirrel 12–16   Prince Nymph 12–16
Serendipity 12–16   Shop Vac 14–18
Feather Duster 12–16   Scud 12–16
Zug Bug 12–16
Leeches 8–12 (black and olive) Damsel Nymphs 12 (olive and tan)
Both patterns are important for Hebgen and Quake Lakes.

APPENDIX 3

Recipes for 16 Key Flies

Flies photographed by Doug O'looney

ANTRON CADDIS PUPA

HOOK   Tiemco 5210, sizes 14–16 or
       Tiemco 100, sizes 14–18

THREAD 8/0 uni-thread, olive
       or brown

BODY   Antron dubbing, green,
       black, olive, gold

HEAD   Rough dubbed of hare's ear
       or Australian opossum in
       tan or brown

The Antron Caddis is a great smooth water caddis
imitation. Versatile, easy to tie and effective.

CHAOS HOPPER

HOOK   Tiemco 2312, sizes 8–14

THREAD 8/0 uni-thread, rusty dun
       or gray

BODY   Tan or gray fly foam

LEGS   Square yellow rubber legs
       and brown hackle

WING   Pale yellow or tan Zelon

DEEP SPARKLE PUPA

HOOK   TMC 100 (standard
         dry fly), sizes 8–12

THREAD   Black

WEIGHT   Non-lead wire (optional)

OVERBODY Half sparkle yarn and
         half fur (chopped very
         fine and mixed in blender;
         touch dubbed sparse and
         fuzzy to the thread)

WING PADS Soft hackle fibers on
          each side of overbody

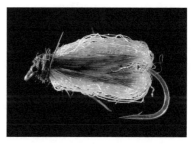

Also tie in brown/bright green, brown/yellow, light ginger (cream thread),
and dark gray to cover 80 percent of the situations you may encounter.

DIVING BLUE-WINGED OLIVE EGG-LAYER

HOOK Tiemco 3769, sizes 14–22 or
Tiemco 760TC, sizes 14–20

THREAD Olive, 8/0

WEIGHT One strip of fine non-
lead wire or bismuth
wire under the thorax

TAILS Medium dun
hackle fibers

ABDOMEN Olive synthetic
dubbing

THORAX Olive synthetic
dubbing (thicker)

WING Clear Antron fibers tied back at a 45-degree angle

HACKLE Medium dun hackle fibers (beard style)

DOUBLE WING, Orange

(use at sunrise and sunset and in autumn)

HOOK TMC 100 (standard dry fly),
sizes 8–16

THREAD Black

TAIL Burnt orange sparkle
yarn stub (combed-out)

TIP White floss

REAR WING Brown elk hair

BODY HACKLE Brown rooster
(palmered and clipped
flat top and bottom)

BODY Burnt orange sparkle
yarn (touch dubbed
rough and fuzzy)

FRONT WING White calf tail

HACKLE Grizzly

Also tie in **Lime** (lime green tail/white tip/lime green rear wing/olive grizzly body hackle/lime green body/white front wing/grizzly hackle) for midday and around green vegetation; **Gray** (dark gray tail/white tip/rust rear wing/cree body hackle/dark gray body/white front wing/grizzly hackle) for overcast days; **Yellow** (yellow tail/white tip/pale yellow rear wing/golden badger body hackle/yellow body/white front wing/grizzly hackle) for rainy conditions; **Royal** (green tail/red tip/brown rear wing/coachman brown body hackle/peacock herl body/white front wing/coachman brown hackle) for sunny days; **Pink Lady** (pink tail/white tip/gray rear wing, dark ginger body hackle/pink body/white front wing/dark ginger hackle) for early mornings and late afternoons; **White** (white tail, tip, rear wing/silver badger body hackle/white body, front wing/grizzly hackle) for shade, at dusk, or as a searcher.

EMERGENT SPARKLE PUPA

HOOK TMC 100 (standard dry fly), sizes 8–12

THREAD Match fly color

OVERBODY Sparkle yarn

UNDERBODY Half sparkle yarn and half fur (chopped fine for dubbing blend)

WING Deer hair

HEAD Dubbed fur or wrapped marabou fibers

Tie in same colors as the Deep Sparkle Pupa.

FLEX-STONE

HOOK TMC 80B (flex hook), sizes 6–8

THREAD Black

TAIL Two rubber strands (tied split)

BODY HACKLE Rooster hackle (palmered over the body and clipped)

BODY Synthetic seal's fur (dubbed rough)

LEGS Six rubber strands (three on each side; not overly long)

WING Elk Hair

HEAD Balsa, deer hair, foam, or hackle of any color

The main colors are **Orange** (white rubber tail/brown legs/orange body hackle/brown elk hair body) and **Ginger** (yellow tail/dark ginger legs/cream body hackle/light tan elk hair body).

FLY FUR STREAMER, RAINBOW AND BROWN TROUT FRY

HOOK Tiemco 106TC, size 8

THREAD 6/0 uni-thread (white for rainbow, red or orange for brown trout)

BODY AND UNDERWING Rust and blonde for brown trout, light blue and tan for rainbow trout fry

HACKLE Mallard flank for rainbow only, or omit

EYES Gold bead chain eyes for brown trout (optional)

Tied with material called "Fly Fur" this pattern has an unbelievable lifelike action in the water. From Nick Nicklas of Blue Ribbon Flies.

IMPROVED X CADDIS

HOOK	Tiemco 100 or 5210, all sizes
THREAD	8/0 uni-thread, rusty dun or olive
SHUCK	Caddis amber or caddis gold dyed Zelon
BODY	Tan, amber, or gold Antron dubbing ribbed with a single strand of Krystal Flash
WING	Underwing of white Zelon, topped with a main wing of caribou or deer hair
HEAD	Match body or hare's mask may be substituted

From Dan and Doug Dauffel who customized our original X Caddis.

IRIS CADDIS

HOOK	Tiemco 102Y, sizes 13–17 or Tiemco 100 and 5210, sizes 14–18
THREAD	8/0 uni-thread, olive or rusty dun
SHUCK	Caddis amber or caddis gold dyed Zelon
BODY	Loop dubbed hare's mask, or pale green, amber, or brown Antron dubbing
EMERGING WINGS	A loop of gray or white Zelon
HEAD	Rough dubbed natural hare's mask

Imitates the most important species of *Hydropsyche* caddis emerging on the Madison River during the summer months.

LITTLE YELLOW OR AMBER STONE BEADHEAD

HOOK	Tiemco 2487, sizes 12–16
THREAD	8/0 uni-thread, yellow
TAILS	Brown stripped goose
LEGS	Brown stripped goose
BODY	Amber or yellow Antron dubbing, gold bead
RIB	Fine gold or copper wire
WING CASE	Brown turkey quill

Pattern goes beyond the traditional use of the bead, incorporating it in a blend of fur, feather, and metal. Great early and late season nymph on the Madison.

NATURAL DRIFT STONEFLY NYMPH

HOOK	TMC 5262, 2X heavy and 2X long nymph, sizes 4–8
THREAD	Black
WEIGHT	Non-lead wire (over rear half of hook shank)
TAIL	Two pheasant tail or turkey feather fibers (split)
RIB	Stripped brown hackle quill
ABDOMEN	Dark brown fur (dubbed)
THORAX	Black deer hair (spun)
HACKLE	Furnace rooster (palmered snugly through thorax hair)

NATURE STONE

HOOK	Tiemco 205BL, sizes 8–10 or Tiemco 5263, sizes 4–8
THREAD	6/0 uni-thread, black
TAILS	Brown or amber dyed goose quills
RIB	#21 or #18 Swannundaze
BELLY	Fluorescent orange yarn
ABDOMEN	Black wool underbody, overwrapped with rough dubbed body of black Australian opossum and rabbit with spiky guard hairs left in

WING CASE	Pronotum and head – dyed latex cut to shape
LEGS	Pheasant back feathers wound one turn over thorax
THORAX	Same as abdomen, over a lead wire foundation
ANTENNAE	Dyed brown or amber goose quills

This pattern looks difficult to tie but it is not. It is well worth the effort to learn this pattern for its durability and effectiveness. I've taken 40 trout on one fly!

SPARKLE DUN

HOOK	Tiemco 5210, sizes 10–16 or Tiemco 100, sizes 10–24
THREAD	8/0 uni-thread to match body color of natural
TAIL (SHUCK)	Olive and mayfly brown Zelon or micro Zelon (for flies size 18 and smaller). Olive or gray for Blue-Winged Olives, mayfly brown for Pale Morning Duns and others.
BODY	Natural or synthetic dubbing (rabbit or beaver fur works well)
WING	Deer hair dyed dun (natural mottled deer for Speckled Spinner and white deer or antelope for White Wing Black)

Body colors and sizes to match mayflies: **Pale Morning Dun** yellowish orange/16–20, **Tiny Western Olive** grayish olive/18–22, **Small Green Drake** dark olive/14–16, **White Wing Black** black/18–22, **Speckled Spinner** tan/16, **Mahogany Dun** deep mahogany/16, **Blue-Winged Olive** dark olive/16–18.

This fly was developed at Blue Ribbon Flies in the late 1970s. It's effective around the world for imitating crippled-impaired mayfly duns of all species that become trapped in their nymphal shucks as they attempt to emerge. Easy to tie, durable, and floats well.

SUNKEN STONE

HOOK Tiemco 5212 or 5262, sizes 4–8

THREAD 6/0 uni-thread, orange or yellow

TAIL Short tuft of black Zelon

BODY Rabbit or other rough dubbing
(range for Salmon Fly, gold for Golden Stone)

WING Five or six clumps of deer hair spaced evenly along the hook shank

Fly floats well but often larger trout prefer a sunken fly.
We purposely pull this fly below the surface where it
often brings a vicious take from huge trout.
From Blue Ribbon's Nick Nicklas.

WOOLHEAD SCULPIN

HOOK Tiemco 300, sizes 2–8

THREAD 6/0 uni-thread, brown or olive

BODY Olive or brown wool yarn

RIB Gold wire

WING Strip of rabbit fur, olive or brown

FINS Sharptail grouse, dyed olive

COLLAR & HEAD Clumps of wool bound to the hook shank and trimmed
(mottle head using different colors of wool; e.g. olive, brown, and gray)

Because sculpins are the most common bait fish
on the Madison River, an appropriate imitation
is a must in your streamer box. This is the best fly
we've found to imitate sculpins.

APPENDIX 4

The Future: Final Thoughts and Notes

*T*he future of the Madison River is bright. Most anglers feel that fishing has never been better on the river. The Madison's wild trout population has rebounded nicely from its record low census figures in the mid-1990s. The rainbow trout count is up again and fisheries biologists are optimistic. A number of things contribute to the continued health of the river. Progressive fisheries programs and research efforts have helped reveal more about whirling disease, low-water stress, angling pressure, fishing during spawning times, and much more. Better educated land managers, anglers, and politicians; stronger strains of wild trout; pollution controls; and greenbelt restrictions prohibiting building on the river's banks all have helped to secure the river's future.

Organizations, including the River Network, Montana Land Reliance, and Montana Nature Conservancy, help secure conservation easements along the Madison that will forever protect wild trout habitat and keep the land intact and free from buildings and harmful development along the river's corridor. Groups, including Trout Unlimited, are working to secure instream flows on the river and key tributaries.

Progressive leaders of agencies, including the National Park Service and the Forest Service, are beginning to recognize the importance of fly fishing when managing our public lands. In their long-range planning documents we now see fishing and wild trout habitat mentioned more often than thousands of tourists or millions of board feet of timber. They close environmentally sensitive areas to protect them from abuse and, in doing so, they often come under attack from special interest groups that want to see these lands and river areas open to every use, no matter what the cost to the environment and its wild inhabitants. Without their courageous stances our sport would suffer irreparable damage. Stand up for these leaders, send them a letter of support and let them know how they are doing.

Groups, including the Yellowstone Park Foundation, Greater Yellowstone Coalition, Whirling Disease Foundation, and Montana Trout Foundation are protecting and preserving wild trout habitat through their persistent and valiant efforts. Without their support wild trout, and fishing for them, would suffer. Step up to the plate and support them, too.

The more we allow the elimination of wet and wild places, the less we are able, in good faith, to pick up rod and reel and take to the waters that are left. And in the end we will be remembered not so much for what we built and developed but for what we protected and refused to destroy. It's our time to see that the wild Madison River and its trout are always protected for future generations.

If you would like to support these efforts, write to:

River Network
44 N. Last Chance Gulch, Rm. 4
Helena, MT 59601

Montana Land Reliance
107 West Lawrence
Helena, MT 59601

Nature Conservancy of Montana
32 S. Ewing
Helena, MT 59601

Yellowstone Park Foundation
37 E. Main St.
Bozeman, MT 59715

Greater Yellowstone Coalition
P.O. Box 1874
Bozeman, MT 59771

Whirling Disease Foundation
P.O. Box 327
Bozeman, MT 59771

Montana Trout Foundation
P.O. Box 1085
Bozeman, MT 59771

Montana Trout Unlimited
P.O. Box 7186
Missoula, MT 59807

SUGGESTED READING

he books listed here are a few I've used to develop effective strategies for fly-fishing the Madison River. They are all wonderful reads in themselves.

BOOKS

Back, Howard. *The Waters of Yellowstone with Rod and Fly*. New York: Dodd, Mead, and Co., 1938; New York: Lyons Press, 2000.

Bergman, Ray. *Trout*. Lanham, Maryland: Derrydale Press, 2000.

Brooks, Charles E. *Fishing Yellowstone Waters*. New York: Lyons & Burford, 1984.

———. *Larger Trout for the Western Fly Fisherman*. Cranbury, New Jersey: A. S. Barnes and Co., 1970.

———. *The Living River*. New York: Lyons and Burford, 1979.

———. *Nymph Fishing for Larger Trout*. New York: Crown Publishers, 1976.

———. *The Trout and the Stream*. New York: Lyons and Burford, 1974.

Brooks, Joe. *Trout Fishing*. New York: Times Mirror Magazines, Inc., 1972.

Harding, Col. E. W. *The Fly Fisher and the Trout's Point of View*. Philadelphia: J. B. Lippincott Co., 1931.

Juracek, John, and Craig Mathews. *Fishing Yellowstone Hatches*. West Yellowstone, Montana: Blue Ribbon Flies, 1992.

Knopp, Malcolm, and Robert Cormier. *Mayflies: A Trout Angler's Study of Trout Water Ephemeroptera*. Helena, Montana: Greycliff Publishing Company, 1997.

LaBranche, George M. L. *The Dry Fly and Fast Water*. New Ed. Helena, Montana: Greycliff Publishing Company, 1998.

LaFontaine, Gary. *Caddisflies*. New York: Lyons and Burford, 1981.

———. *The Dry Fly, New Angles*. Helena, Montana: Greycliff Publishing Company, 1990.

———. *Fly Fishing the Mountain Lakes*. Helena, Montana: Greycliff Publishing Company, 1998.

———. *Trout Flies: Proven Patterns*. Helena, Montana: Greycliff Publishing Company, 1993.

Lyons, Nick. *Bright Rivers*. New York: J. B. Lippincot Co., 1977.

———. *Spring Creek*. New York: Atlantic Monthly Press, 1992.

135

Mathews, Craig, and Clayton Molinero. *The Yellowstone Fly-Fishing Guide*. New York: Lyons and Burford, 1997.

Mathews, Craig, and John Juracek. *Fly Patterns of Yellowstone*. West Yellowstone, Montana: Blue Ribbon Flies, 1987.

Mathews, Craig. *Western Fly-Fishing Strategies*. New York: Lyons Press, 1998.

Roemhild, George. *Aquatic Insects of Yellowstone*. Mammoth, Wyoming: Yellowstone Institute, 1983.

Schwiebert, Ernest. *Nymphs*. New York: Winchester Press, 1973.

Swisher, Doug, and Carl Richards. *Fly Fishing Strategy*. New York: Crown Publisher, 1975.

Varley, John, and Paul Schullery. *Freshwater Wilderness*. Mammoth, Wyoming: Yellowstone Library and Museum Association, 1983.

Walker, Richard. *Trout Fishing*. North Pomfret, Vermont: David & Charles Publishers, 1982.

AUDIO TAPE

Mathews, Craig, and Gary LaFontaine. *Fly-Fishing the Madison River*. River Rap Series. Helena, Montana: Greycliff Publishing Company, 1986.

INDEX

137

ANGLER'S NOTES

ABOUT THE AUTHORS

RAIG MATHEWS

Craig Mathews has fished, developed fly patterns for, guided on, and studied the Madison River for more than 30 years. He has written dozens of articles for major fly-fishing publications on fly-fishing the Madison River and other waters in Montana, Idaho, and Yellowstone National Park, and he is author and co-author of five books on fly-fishing western states and the Yellowstone area, including *Fly Patterns of Yellowstone, Fishing Yellowstone Hatches, The Yellowstone Fly-Fishing Guide, Western Fly-Fishing Strategies,* and *Fly-Fishing the Madison River.*

The former police chief, with his wife Jackie, founded Blue Ribbon Flies in West Yellowstone, Montana, in 1979. Blue Ribbon Flies has won several awards, including the Nature Conservancy's Business Conservation Award for working to preserve wild trout habitat, and the Greater Yellowstone Coalition's highest honor for exemplifying business efforts to preserve, protect, and enhance the Greater Yellowstone Ecosystem and its wild trout. In 1997 Yellowstone National Park presented Craig and Jackie with the prestigious Yellowstone Protector Award for their business efforts to preserve and protect Yellowstone National Park. Craig is currently working with River Network to protect a mile and a half of the Madison River from harmful streamside development and keep it open to the public forever.

ARY LaFONTAINE

Nationally known and respected fly-fishing guru Gary LaFontaine has fished and guided on the Madison River for twenty-plus years. His award-winning and widely acclaimed books include *The Dry Fly: New Angles, Trout Flies: Proven Patterns, Fly Fishing the Mountain Lakes,* and *Caddisflies,* and he has written innumerable magazine articles for fly-fishing publications. He was named Angler of the Year in 1996 by *Fly Rod & Reel.* He lives in Montana with his dogs, Chester and Zeb.